A New Wedding Service for You

ARTHUR HOMBURG, EDITOR

NINETEEN ORDERS OF WORSHIP FOR THE
PROSPECTIVE BRIDE AND GROOM

C.S.S. Publishing Company, Inc.
Lima, Ohio

A NEW WEDDING SERVICE FOR YOU

Second Printing 1985
Third Printing 1986
Fourth Printing 1989

5815/ISBN 0-89536-731-9

PRINTED IN U.S.A.

This book is dedicated to the many couples over the past ten years who, while I was counseling them for marriage, took time and invested the energy, to write their own services.

A special word of thanks to our church secretary, Shirley Ness, who re-typed all the wedding services.

Preface

In 1973, during a pre-marriage counseling session when it came time to go over the traditional wedding service with the couple, the young woman asked, "Is this the only choice we have for a wedding service?" I answered "This is it!"

She said, "But it's so old — and it doesn't say what we would like to have said at our wedding!" I replied "Well, then why don't you write your own?"

The young woman said, "But we wouldn't even know where to begin." I said, "I'll help you."

We began by talking about what marriage is all about, and what parts a marriage service must have. I told them that any scripture lesson they desired could be included along with any other poem or literature that would be meaningful to them — so long as it was compatable with Christian faith. I indicated that they could write their own vows and their own prayers.

Over a period of months, their wedding service evolved. It became the first of many that couples and I would write together. This book includes nineteen of them.

Not every couple wants to write their own service, and not every couple could. The couples that have written their own have included thoughtful individuals who displayed a deep Christian faith, and who were open to planning their wedding many months in advance. If I meet with a couple six months to a year in advance of their wedding date, I will suggest the writing of their own service.

After I got into the process of writing wedding services with couples, I found that they needed to see a sample wedding service written by another couple. I began making copies of others that had been written. Sometimes the new couple would only need to change the placement of parts. Other times they would want only to change the vows. Other times they would want to add other scripture lessons and writings.

But what the writing — or altering — of services did for the couple was to allow them to make the service their own. They had to wrestle with the meaning of each part and how it applied to them personally. They had to work through what it means to be married in the church and to make their vows before God.

This book of wedding services includes a variety of vows, scripture readings, prayers, and meditations. Each service is unique. The services can be used as they are. Or, parts can be taken from the various services to make still another wedding service. When this is done, the service then belongs to the couple.

1

Unique characteristics in this ceremony:

The service is very traditional in format with the exception of the more intimate prayer at the beginning and the lighting of the unity candle

Originally compiled by my associate pastor, Andy Sedlins, this ceremony has been used many times. Occasionally, a couple will make alterations, such as the addition of other prayers, a different blessing for the rings, or the inclusion of writings meaningful to them.

The Marriage Service of ______________ and ______________ on ______________ .

In the Name of the Father, and of the Son, and of the Holy Spirit. Amen (Congregation seated)

Dear Friends: We have come together in the presence of God to witness and bless the joining together of ______________ and ______________ in the holy relationship of marriage. The union of husband and wife in heart, body, and mind is intended by God for their mutual joy; for the help and comfort given one another in prosperity and adversity; and, when it is God's will, for the procreation of children and their nurture in the knowledge and love of the Lord. Therefore marriage is not to be entered into unadvisedly or lightly, but reverently, deliberately, and in accordance with the purposes for which it was instituted by God.

Prayer: Let us pray: Out of this tangled world, O God. You have drawn together these two persons and are binding them firmly by the sure insights of love. We thank you for the homes in which ______________ and ______________ have been nurtured in the formative years of their lives; for parents who have sacrificed on their behalf and made possible opportunities of education; for the church which has awakened them to the meaning of eternal life.

Our Father, bless these as they come before family, friends, and church to affirm the choice that they have made of each other as a life's mate and their intention to establish a home where your love may be celebrated in the family. Grant them a seriousness of purpose that they may be delivered from empty words and casual commitments. For the fulfilment of their vows, may they discern the varied facets of your many-splendored love. May your Word nurture them all the days of their lives, that their dreams and aspirations for life may find fulfilment in the doing of your will in all things. As we share with them in the celebration of love on this occasion, may we all grow toward the perfection that is experienced in Christ our Lord. Amen.

Listen Now to What the Word of God Teaches Concerning Marriage.

The Lord God Said: "It is not good that the man should be alone; I will make him a helper fit for him." (Genesis 2:18)

Our Lord Jesus Christ Said: From the beginning of creation 'God made them male and female. For this reason a man shall leave his father and mother and be joined to his wife, and the two shall become one.' So they are no longer two but one. What therefore God has joined together, let not man put asunder." (Mark 10:6-9)

The Apostle Paul, speaking by the Holy Spirit says: "Set your hearts on the greater gifts. I will show you the way which surpasses all the others. If I speak in the tongues of men and of angels, but have not love, I am a noisy gong or a clanging cymbal. And if I have prophetic powers, and understand all mysteries and all knowledge, and if I have all faith, so as to move mountains, but have not love, I am nothing. If I give away all I have, and if I deliver my body to be burned, but have not love, I gain nothing. Love is patient and kind; love is not jealous or boastful; it is not arrogant or rude. Love does not insist on its own way; it is not irritable or resentful; it does not rejoice at wrong, but rejoices in the right. Love bears all things, hopes all things, endures all things. Love never fails." (1 Corinthians 12:31-13:8)

In the First Letter of John We Read: "Beloved, let us love one another; for love is of God, and he who loves is born of God and knows God. He who does not love does not know God; for God is love. In this the love of God was made manifest among us, that God sent his only Son into the world, so that we might live through him. In this is love, not that we loved God but that he loved us and sent his Son to be the expiation for our sins. Beloved, if God so loved us, we also ought to love one another. No man has ever seen God; if we love one another, God abides in us and his love is perfected in us." (1 John 4:7-12)

The Lord God in his goodness created us male and female, and by the gift of marriage founded human community in a joy that begins now, and is brought to perfection in the life to come. Because of sin, our age-old rebellion, the gladness of marriage can be overcast and the gift of the family can become a burden. But because God, who established marriage, continues still to bless it with his abundant and ever-present support, we can be sustained in our weariness and have our joy restored.

These two, who have previously traveled separate ways, come now to be made one.

______________, will you have this woman to be your wife, to live together, in the holy relationship of marriage? Will you love her, comfort her, honor and support her in joy and in suffering, and forsaking all others, remain with her as long as you both shall live? (Groom: I will)

______________, will you have this man to be your husband, to live together, in the holy relationship of marriage? Will you love him, comfort him, honor and support him in joy and in suffering, and forsaking all others, remain with him as long as you both shall live? (Bride: I will)

Who gives this woman to be married to this man? (Father: Her mother and I)

Join right hands — face each other:

I, ______________, take you, ______________, to be my wife/ to have and to hold/ from this day forward/ for better for worse/ for richer for poorer/ in sickness and in health/ to love and to cherish/ until we are parted by death./ This is my solemn vow.

I, ______________, take you, ______________, to be my husband/ to have and to hold from this day forward/ for better for worse/ for richer for poorer/ in sickness and in health/ to love and to cherish/ until we are parted by death./ This is my solemn vow.

Rings:I give you this ring/ as a sign of my love and faithfulness.

Join right hands

Now that ______________ and ______________ have given themselves to each other by solemn vows, with the joining of hands and the giving and receiving of a ring, I pronounce that they are husband and wife, in the name of the Father, and of the Son and of the Holy Spirit. Those whom God has joined together let no one put asunder. Amen.

Candle Ceremony: ______________ and ______________ now symbolize their union by lighting a common candle as a sign that they are no longer two, but one. May their love burn bright and may their life together be a light, an example of Christ's love in the world.

Blessing: The Lord God, who created our first parents and established them in marriage, establish and sustain you, that you may find delight in each other and grow in holy love until your life's end. Amen.

Prayers: Let us pray: Father of love, shower your grace upon this couple who have come before you to pledge themselves to live together in marriage. Give them wisdom and devotion in the ordering of their common life, that each may be to the other a strength in need, a counselor in perplexity, a comfort in sorrow, and a companion in joy. Give them grace, when they hurt each other, to recognize and acknowledge their fault, and to seek each other's forgiveness and yours. Give them such fulfillment of their mutual affection that they may reach out in love and concern for others. Grant that all married persons who have witnessed these vows may find their lives
strengthened and their loyalties confirmed.

The Lord's Prayer

The Lord bless you and keep you. The Lord make his face shine upon you and be gracious to you. The Lord look upon you with favor and give you peace. Amen.

May the Father, Son and Holy Spirit direct and keep you in trust and love all the days of your life. Amen

2

Unique characteristics in this ceremony:

This service begins with a brief meditation on marriage. The scripture lesson from 1 Corinthians, the thirteenth chapter, is in modern language.
The exchanging of the vows and rings are blended together into one act. The vows are intimate and meaningful, and the rings truly become a symbol of the vows exchanged.

The Marriage Service of ______________ and ______________ on ______________ .

In the name of the Father and of the Son and of the Holy Spirit. (Congregation seated)

On this occasion ______________ and ______________ come before family, friends, and the church to affirm the choice that they have made of each other as life's mates and their intention to establish a home for the raising of a family and the fulfillment of life together

As the years go by ______________ and ______________ , you will realize that this marriage you have chosen for yourselves was not given to you by anyone else. It has been, and must continue to be, a process that builds throughout your lives. You must work at marriage day by day . . . meeting the disappointments, as well as the joys, that your lives together will bring. We have gathered this afternoon with you, to help you give added strength to this marriage. But, in doing this, we realize that this outward act of the marriage service is but a symbol of that which is inward and real; a union of two people . . . which God blesses in the church, and the state makes legal. Marriage is a union by your own free choice . . . with the full knowledge of what that choice means . . . when two people give themselves to each other . . . in love for the rest of their lives.

The quality of love that is necessary for marriage has been described for us by St. Paul in the thirteenth chapter of 1 Corinthians:

I may speak in tongues of men or of angels, but if I am without love, I am a sounding gong or a clanging cymbal. I may have the gift of prophecy, and know every hidden truth: I may have faith strong enough to move mountains: But if I have no love, I am nothing. I may dole out all I possess, or even give my body to be burned, but if I have no love, I am none the better.

Love is patient: Love is kind and envies no one. Love is never boastful, nor conceited, nor rude: Never selfish, not quick to take offence. Love keeps no score of wrongs: Does not gloat over other's sins, but delights in the truth. There is nothing love cannot face: There is no limit to its faith, its hope, and its endurance.

Love never ends . . . are there prophets? Their work will be over. Are there outbursts of ecstacy? They will cease. Is there knowledge? It will vanish away: For our knowledge and our prophecy are but partial, and the partial vanishes when wholeness comes. When I was a child, my speech, my outlook, and my thoughts were all childish. Then I grew up and I had finished with childish things. Now we see only puzzling reflections in a mirror, but then we shall see face to face. In a word . . . there are three things that last forever: Faith,Hope, and Love, but the greatest of them all is love.

Who gives this woman to be married to this man?

And are you ______________ and ______________ , now ready in the presence of your family and friends to declare your intention to make this venture of faith and love in marriage?

______________, are you willing to receive ______________ as your wife having confidence that your abiding faith and love in each other will last forever? (Answer: I am)

______________ , are you willing to receive ______________ as your husband, having full confidence that your abiding faith and love in each other will last forever? (Answer: I am)

To the Altar

Let us pray: Heavenly Father, who has endowed us with creative ability in love, we present to you ______________ and ______________ for your blessing upon their marriage. May you endow their union with true devotion, spiritual commitment, and personal integrity.

Eternal God, give ______________ and ______________ the grace to keep the bond of union between them. When selfishness shows itself, grant generosity; when mistrust is a temptation, give moral strength; where misunderstanding intrudes, give patience and gentleness. When suffering becomes their lot, give them a strong faith and abiding hope. In Christ's name. Amen

Marriage requires much generosity . . . unselfishness . . . flexibility . . . and forbearance from both husband and wife. The reality and happiness of your marriage depends upon the inner experience of your heart and the integrity of your commitment.

Rings: As a seal of your promise, you have chosen rings of precious metal, symbolizing the unity, wholeness and endlessness of your life together.

Will you, _______________ , place this ring upon the wedding finger of your bride and say your promise to her.

"I, _______________, take you, _______________ , to be the wife of all my days. To be the mother of our children, to be the companion of our home. We shall keep together what share of sorrow our lives may lay upon us. And we shall hold together our store of goodness and of love.

Take this ring, freely given, as a token of my love and a symbol of my intention to live with you in love and respect. As this ring has no end, neither shall my love for you."

Will you, _______________ , place this ring upon the wedding finger of your groom and say your promise to him.

"I, _______________ , take you, _______________ , to be the husband of all my days. To be the father of our children, to be the companion of our home. We shall keep together what share of sorrow our lives may lay upon us. And we shall hold together our store of goodness and of love. Take this ring, freely given, as a token of my love and as a symbol of my intention to live with you in love and respect. As this ring has no end, neither shall my love for you."

And now symbolic of the fact that your two lives have become one, light the wedding candle.

Join right hands.

Since you, _______________ and _______________ , have consented together to be married and have witnessed the same before God and this community of relatives and friends and have committed your love and faith to each other and have sealed your promises with rings, I announce that God has made you husband and wife, in the name of the Father and of the Son and of the Holy Spirit. What God has joined together, let no one put asunder. Amen

Kneel.

Blessing: The Lord God, who created our first parents and established their union in marriage, establish, sustain and bless you, that you may find delight in each other and grow in holy love until your life's end. Amen

Let us pray: Father of love, shower your grace upon

______________ and ______________ who have come before you and pledged themselves to live together in holy marriage. Give them wisdom and devotion in the ordering of their common life, that each may be to the other a strength in need . . . a counselor in perplexity . . . a comfort in sorrow . . . and a companion in joy. Give them such fulfillment of their mutual affection that they may reach out in love and concern for others. Grant that all married persons who have witnessed these vows may find their lives strengthened and their loyalties confirmed. In Christ's Name. Amen

Benediction: May the Father, Son, and Holy Spirit direct and keep you in trust and love all the days of your life. Amen

Arise and kiss the bride.

I introduce to you for the first time: Mr. and Mrs. ______________ ______________!

3

Unique characteristics in this ceremony:

The statement of intention in this service is shortened and emphasizes the couple's love for and faith in each other. The response is "I Am," instead of "I Do," or "I Will."

Following the exchange of vows and rings, and before the pronouncement of marriage, there is included the writing of Kahlil Gibran, from ***The Prophet,*** *which speaks of the marriage partner's individuality in their union.*

The marriage service of ____________ and ____________ on ____________

Call to Worship: In the name of the Father, the Son and the Holy Spirit. Amen (Congregation seated)

Tonight, the family and friends of ____________ and ____________ have come to witness their union in marriage and to ask for God's blessings on the lives that they wish to share.

Let us pray: O God, who alone unites persons in holy bonds of covenant, without whose spirit there is no abiding unity, be present in the inner being of these who have come to witness their promise to each other — in the Spirit of Christ, the Lord. Amen

Declaration of Intention: The resourcefulness of Christian love has been declared by the Apostle Paul in these unforgettable words: Love is patient and kind; love is not jealous or boastful; it is not arrogant or rude. Love does not insist on its own way; it is not irritable or resentful; it does not rejoice at wrong but rejoices in the right. Love bears all things, believes all things, hopes all things. All else may pass away but love never ends. (1 Corinthians 13)

Love enriches each part of life and marriage enriches love. Marriage should be a union of two individuals; a decision to share two lives in the kind of Christian love described by Apostle Paul.

Two lives, shared, can hold more fulfillment and happiness than either life alone, but a commitment to each sharing requires great love and faith.

______________ , are you ready to enter into marriage with ______________ , believing that the love you share and your faith in each other will endure all things?

Groom: I am.

______________ , are you ready to enter into marriage with ______________, believing that the love you share and your faith in each other will endure all things?

Bride: I am.

Symbolic Approval: Who will bless this marriage in behalf of the families and friends of ______________ and ______________ ?

Father: ______________ mother and I.

(To altar.)

Prayer: Let us pray.

Out of this tangled world, O God, you have drawn together these two people and are binding them firmly by the sure insights of love. We thank you for the homes in which ______________ and ______________ have lived, for parents who have supported them and encouraged them even in the most trying times and who have sacrificed in their behalf and made great opportunities possible. We also thank you for the friendships they have enjoyed and for the church which has awakened them to the meaning of eternal life.

Our Father, bless these as they come before family, friends, and church to affirm the choice that they have made of each other. As we share with them in the celebration of love on this occasion, may we all grow toward the perfection that is experienced in your love. We pray in the spirit of the love of Christ. Amen

Vows: ______________ and ______________ , will you join your right hands, face each other and repeat individually after me:

(Groom) ______________ , I take you to be my wife, from this moment on. I vow to give and to receive, to speak and to listen, to inspire and to respond, to respect and to cherish, and to work with you to achieve the goals and dreams of our lives.

(Bride) ______________ , I take you to be my husband, from this moment on. I vow to give and to receive, to speak and to listen, to inspire and to respond, to respect and to cherish and to work with you to achieve the goals and dreams of our lives.

Exchange of Rings: These rings are a symbol of wedded love. As often as either of you see them, you will be reminded of this high moment and the endless love you promise.

(To Groom) Take this ring and place it on ______________ finger and repeat: This ring, I give to you, in token and pledge of our constant faith and abiding love.

(To Bride) Take this ring and place it on ____________ finger and repeat: This ring, I give to you, in token and pledge of our constant faith and abiding love.

Light unity candle, then kneel.

Reading:

You were born together and together you shall be forevermore.
You shall be together when the white wings of death scatter your days.
Ay, you shall be together even in the silent memory of God.
But let there be spaces in your togetherness,
And let the winds of the heavens dance between you.

Love one another but make not a bond of love:
Let it rather be a moving sea between the shores of your souls.
Fill each other's cup but drink not from one cup.
Give one another of your bread but eat not from the same loaf.
Sing and dance together and be joyous, but let each one of you be alone.
Even as the strings of a lute are alone though they quiver with the same music.

Give your hearts, but not into each other's keeping.
For only the hand of Life can contain your hearts.
And stand together yet not too near together.
For the pillars of the temple stand apart.
And the oak tree and the cypress grow not in each other's shadow.*

Announcement of Marriage: (Join right hands.)

____________ and ____________, since you have promised your love to each other and before God and these witnesses have exchanged these solemn vows, and these symbols of genuine and undying love, I announce that God has made you husband and wife.

Now may God's joy which the world cannot give, and which the world cannot take away, be yours today and tomorrow and in all of life's tomorrows. In the name of the Father and of the Son and of the Holy Spirit. Amen

Kiss the bride!

*Reprinted from *The Prophet*, by Kahlil Gibran, by permission of Alfred A. Knopf, Inc.

4

Unique characteristics in this ceremony:

The story of God's creation of woman from the second chapter of Genesis is the initial Scripture lesson in this service. The exchanging of vows and rings are again combined, but the vows are of a more traditional variety. Following the exchange of vows and rings and pronouncement of marriage, the Scripture lesson from 1 Corinthians 13 is read.

The marriage service of ______________ and ______________ on ______________

Invocation: In the name of the Father, the Son, and the Holy Spirit. Amen

Marriage is as old as the human family. It is the highest of life's relationships. It is of the ordaining of the Creator in the very nature of our being as man and as woman. God's fatherly intention toward his children is revealed through this relationship. A relationship so sacred must not be entered into casually, but thoughtfully and deliberately.

On this occasion ______________ and ______________ come before family, friends, and church to affirm the choice that they have made of each other as life's mate and their intention to establish a home for the raising of a family and the fulfilment of life together.

Who gives this woman to be married to this man?

Father: Her mother and I do.

(Genesis 2:18, 2:21-24) The Lord God said, "It is not good that the man should be alone; I will make him a helper fit for him." So the Lord God caused a deep sleep to fall upon the man, and while he slept took one of his ribs and closed up its place with flesh, and the rib which the Lord God had taken from the man he made into a woman and brought her to the man. Then the man said, "This at last is bone of my bone and flesh of my flesh; she shall be called Woman, because she was taken out of Man." Therefore a man leaves his father and his mother and cleaves to his wife, and they become one.

______________ and ______________ , as you contemplate the

making of your vows to each other, realize that henceforth your destinies shall be woven of one design and your perils and your joys shall not be known apart. The words "I love you," first spoken shyly in months gone by, when it was not known if they would be accepted or returned in kind, are today spoken in the full commitment of yourselves to each other.

Prayer: (Kneel) Let us pray: Out of this tangled world, O God, you have drawn together these two persons and are binding them firmly in marriage. We thank you for the homes in which _______________ and _______________ have been nurtured in the formative years of their lives; for parents who have sacrificed in their behalf and made possible opportunities for education and growth; for the church which has awakened them to the meaning of eternal life. Our Father, bless these your children, now and always. May they ever remain as happy and united as they now are as they kneel at your altar, asking for your holy blessing. May your Word nurture them all the days of their lives, that their dreams and aspirations for life may find fulfilment in the doing of your will in all things. As we share with them in the celebration of love on this occasion, may we all grow toward the perfection that is experienced in your love. In Jesus' name we pray. Amen

Vows: Do you, _______________ , take this woman to thy wedded wife, to live together after God's ordinance in the holy estate of matrimony? Wilt thou love her, comfort her, honor and keep her in sickness and in health, and, forsaking all others, keep thee only unto her, as long as you both shall live?

Groom: "I do."

Do you, _______________ , take this man to thy wedded husband, to live together after God's ordinance in the holy estate of matrimony? Wilt thou love him, comfort him, honor and keep him in sickness and in health, and forsaking all others, keep thee only unto him, as long as you both shall live?

Bride: "I do."

(To altar)

Rings: (To groom) _______________ , take _______________ by the left hand, and placing the ring upon her wedding finger, repeat after me:

I, _______________ , take thee, _______________ , to my wedded wife, to have and to hold from this day forward, for better, for worse, for richer, for poorer, in sickness and in health, to love and to cherish, till death us do part, according to the will of God.

(To bride) ______________ , take ______________ by his left hand, and placing the ring upon his wedding finger, repeat after me:

I, ______________ , take thee, ______________ , to my wedded husband, to have and to hold from this day forward, for better, for worse, for richer, for poorer, in sickness and in health, to love and to cherish, till death us do part, according to God's holy ordinance.

And now symbolic of your lives having become one — will you light the Wedding Candle?

(Join right hands.)

Forasmuch as ______________ and ______________ have consented together in holy wedlock, and have declared the same before God and these witnesses, I pronounce them husband and wife. In the name of the Father, and of the Son and of the Holy Spirit. Amen

What God has joined together, let not man put asunder.

(Kneel) The Lord God, who created our first parents and established them in marriage, establish and sustain you, that you may find delight in each other, and grow in holy love until your life's end. May you dwell in God's presence forever, may true and constant love preserve you.

Let us pray: Almighty and most merciful God, who hast now united this Man and this Woman in holy matrimony, grant them grace to live therein according to Thy holy Word, strengthen them in constant fidelity, faith, and affection toward each other. In Christ's name. Amen

(1 Corinthians 13:4-7) Love is patient and kind, love is not jealous or boastful; it is not arrogant or rude. Love does not insist on its way; it is not irritable or resentful; it does not rejoice at wrong, but rejoices in the right. Lovve bears all things, believes all things, hopes all things, endures all things. . . . So faith, hope, and love abide, but the greatest of these is Love.

The Lord's Prayer (in unison)

Benediction: (Kneel) The Lord bless thee and keep thee. The Lord make his face shine upon thee and be gracious unto thee. The Lord lift up his countenance upon thee, and grant thee his peace. Amen.

Kiss.

I now present to you Mr. and Mrs. ______________ ______________ .

5

Unique characteristics in this ceremony:

The service was initially used in a second marriage for both the bride and groom. There is remorse over human sin and imperfection, and yet joy in God's forgiveness.

The vows are longer and reflect some deep thought and meditation on what each would in love propose to do for the other.

This ceremony involves participation by the congregation in the psalm at the beginning, and again in another psalm between the lessons. Included is a lesson from the Song of Solomon, which is the response of the Bride to the Bridegroom. The ending prayer is filled with the joy of Christ's goodness and mercy as a shield from sin and strife.

The marriage service of ______________ **and** ______________ **on** ______________ .

The Invocation: We gather together in the Name of God the Father, God the Son, and God the Holy Spirit. May the grace of our Lord Jesus Christ, the Love of God, and the fellowship of the Holy Spirit be with you all. Amen

Prayer of Praise: (By all)

We will sing the story of your love, O Lord
And proclaim your faithfulness forever.
In this place shall be heard again the sounds of joy and gladness,
the voice of the bridegroom and the bride.

Here they offer praise and thanksgiving in the house of the Lord,
and we hear their voice of shouting.
"Praise the Lord of Hosts, for he is good,
For his love endures forever."
Give thanks to him and bless his Name;
The Lord is good, his love is everlasting,
and his faithfulness endures to all generations.

We will sing the story of your love, O Lord,
and proclaim your faithfulness forever.

The Prayer: Eternal God, Father of mankind, as you gladdened the wedding in Cana in Galilee by the presence of your Son, so by his presence now make the occasion of this wedding one of rejoicing. In your favor look upon ______________ and ______________ , about to be joined in marriage, and grant that they, rejoicing in all your gifts, may at length celebrate with Christ the Bridegroom the marriage feast which has no end. Amen

The Scriptures: The Song of Solomon 2:10-13; Psalm 33 (read responsively by all); Ephesians 5:21-33.

The Marriage: The Lord God created mankind male and female and by the gift of marriage founded human community in a joy that begins now and is brought to perfection in the life to come. But because of our sin and man's age-old rebellion, the gladness of marriage can be overcast and the gift of the family can become a burden. Nevertheless, because of his Love God our Father from the beginning established marriage and continues still to bless it with his abundant and ever-present support, we can be sustained in our weariness and have our joy restored.

______________ and ______________ , if it is your intention to share with each other your laughter and your tears and all that the years will bring, by your promises bind yourselves now to each other as husband and wife.

(Face each other and join hands.)

Groom/Bride: I take you, ______________ / ______________ , to be my wife/husband, and these things I promise to you: I will be faithful to you and honest with you; I will respect, trust, help, and care for you. I will give and receive, speak and listen, inspire and respond: I will forgive you as we have been forgiven: and in all circumstances of our life together, I will try with you to better understand ourselves, the world, and our Lord, through the best and the worst of what is to come, that together we may serve God and others as long as we both shall live.

The Exchange of Rings: Groom/Bride: This ring is a sign of my love and faithfulness.

The Lighting of the Wedding Candle: ______________ and ______________ , by their promises before God, have made themselves husband and wife. They have been joined together as one by the Love of God the Father in the light of the Spirit of Christ, and man must not divide them. Blessed by the Father and the Son and the Holy Spirit now and forever.

The Blessing: (Kneel) The Lord God, who created our first parents and established them in marriage, establish and sustain you, that you may find delight in each other and grow in holy love until your life's end. May you dwell in God's presence forever; may true and constant love preserve you.

The Prayer: Creator Father, whose wisdom, love, and power first bound two lives together in Eden, today to these children, ______________ and ______________ , give your earliest gifts: A home made happy by you and a love kept true by you. Savior Jesus, may your overwhelming goodness and grace be always present in their lives. May their earthly gladness be transformed to the heavenly, teaching them that the gift is yours.

Spirit of the Father, breathe on them from above with your pureness and tender love, guarding them by your presence from sin and strife, that their lives may be guided and ruled by you.

Heavenly Father, build their lives together.

Dear Savior, bless their lives with your joy and forgiveness. Holy Spirit, may the love you make holy this day, be an endless love begun. Amen

The Lord's Prayer (By all)

The Benediction: May Almighty God bless you and direct you all the days of your life. Almighty God, Father, Son, and Holy Spirit keep you in his light and truth and love all the days of your life. Amen

6

Unique characteristics in this ceremony:

The thrust of the meditation in this service is that marriage is a process. The prayer at the end speaks of the sacramental nature of marriage.

The benediction is more a prayer than a blessing, which asks God's strength so that the bride and groom may be faithful.

The marriage service of ______________ **and** ______________ **on** ______________ .

In the name of the Father and of the Son, and the Holy Spirit. Amen

Invocation Prayer: Let us pray: O God, who alone unites persons in holy bonds of matrimony, without whose Spirit there is no abiding unity or oneness, be present with ______________ and ______________ and all who have come this afternoon to witness their commitment to each other in the Spirit of the love of Christ. Amen

Symbolic Approval: Who gives this woman to marry this man?

Bride's Father: Her mother and I.

Meditation Concerning Marriage: A wedding is the celebration of the highest we know in love, the pledging of two lives to common goals. On this occasion ______________ and ______________ come before family, friends, and church to affirm the choice that they have made of each other as a life's mate and their intention to establish a home for the raising of a family and the fulfilment of life together.

As the years go by, you will realize that this marriage, you yourselves have chosen, was not given to you by anyone else. It has been, and must continue to be, a process that builds throughout your lives. You must work at it day by day, meeting the disappointments, as well as the joys, that your lives together will bring. We have gathered with you this afternoon to help you give added life to this marriage that you have chosen for yourselves. But, in doing this, we realize that this outward act is but a symbol of that which is inward and real: a union of two people, which a church may bless and the state may make legal, but which neither church nor state can create. It is such a union, by your own free choice — and with full knowledge of what that choice means — that you two have come to live.

Readings from Old Testament: (Genesis 1:26-28, 31a) God said, "Let us make man in our own image, in the likeness of ourselves, and let them be masters of the fish of the sea, the birds of heaven, the cattle, all the wild beasts and all reptiles that crawl upon the earth."

God created man in the image of himself, in the image God he creates him, male and female he created them.

God blessed them, saying to them, "Be fruitful, multiply, fill the earth and conquer it. Be masters of the fish, the birds of heaven and all living animals on the earth."

God saw all he had made, and indeed it was very good.

Reading from New Testament: (Mark 10:6-9) From the beginning of creation God made them male and female.

This is why a man must leave father and mother, and the two become one body. They are no longer two, therefore, but one body.

So then, what God has united, man must not divide.

Sermonette

Exchange of Wedding Vows: (Face each other) Groom: I, _______________, take you, _______________, to be my wedded wife; I promise to be your loving and faithful husband, in prosperity and in need, in joy and in sorrow, in sickness and in health, and to respect your privileges, as an individual, as long as we both shall live.

Bride: I, _______________, take you, _______________, to be my wedded husband; I promise to be your loving and faithful wife, in prosperity and in need, in joy and in sorrow, in sickness and in health, and to respect your privileges as an individual, as long as we both shall live.

Service of Rings: Lord, bless these rings which we bless in your Name. Grant that those who wear them may always have a deep faith in each other. May they do your will and always live together in peace, good will, and love. We ask this through Christ our Lord. Amen

Groom: I give you, _______________, this ring as a symbol of my love and faithfulness.

Bride: I give you, _______________, this ring as a symbol of my love and faithfulness.

Lighting of Candle: (Kneel) My dear friends, let us ask God for his continued blessing upon _______________ and _______________.

Holy Father, creator of the universe, maker of man and woman in your own likeness, source of blessing for married life, we humbly pray to you for this woman, who today is united with her husband in this sacrament of marriage.

May your fullest blessing come upon her and her husband, so that they may together rejoice in your gift of married love and enrich your Church with their children.

Lord, may they both praise you when they are happy and turn to you in their sorrows. May they be glad that you help them in their work and know that you are with them in their need. May they pray to you in the community of the church, and be your witnesses in the world. May they reach old age in the company of their friends, and come at last to the kingdom of heaven.

We ask this through Christ our Lord.

The Lord's Prayer

Benediction: Eternal God: Without your grace no promise is sure. Strengthen ______________ and ______________ with the gift of your Spirit so they may fulfill the vows they have taken. Keep them faithful to each other and to you. Fill them with such love and joy that they may build a home where no one is a stranger. And guide them by your word to serve you all the days of their lives: through Jesus Christ our Lord, to whom be honor and glory forever and ever. Amen

Kiss the bride.

I present to you Mr. and Mrs. ______________ ______________!

7

Unique characteristics in this ceremony:

Following each of the lessons in this service is a meditative explanation of the meaning of the scriptural passage as it applies to marriage. The statement of intention is read by the bride and groom, and each give their response. The vows are memorized and given without the minister giving the words first.

Between the exchange of vows and rings, there is a pastoral admonition given to the couple about the responsibilities they have accepted.

The marriage service of ______________ and ______________ on ______________ .

In the name of the Father and of the Son and of the Holy Spirit. Amen

Let us pray: O God, who alone unites persons in the holy bonds of covenant, without whose Spirit there is no abiding unity or oneness, be present in the inner being of ______________ and ______________ who have come this day to witness to their commitment to each other, in the Spirit of the Love of Christ. Amen

Dear Christian Friends: Since marriage is a part of God's order of creation and is to be honored by his people, let us consider what marriage means, as you, ______________ and ______________ , come together to proclaim in public your devotion and your joint purpose from this time forward, to join yourselves in marriage, and to seek the blessing of God for your marriage.

In the first chapter of Genesis we read: "So God created man in his own image, in the image of God created he him; male and female created he them. And God blessed them and said to them, 'Be fruitful and multiply and replenish the earth and subdue it.' " (Genesis 1:27-28)

This means that it is God's will that a man and a woman live together in his world as images of himself; that he gives them his blessing and charges them with responsibility for each other, for their opportunity as parents, and as responsible persons involved in his created world.

In Matthew we read the words of Jesus: "Have you not read that he who created them male and female from the beginning, said, 'for this reason a man shall leave his father and mother and shall cling to his wife, and the two shall be one. So they are no longer two but one. What therefore God has joined, let no one separate.' " (Matthew 19:4-6)

Christ said that in marriage the two of you shall become one, become one, in spirit and body, one in life-style, one in ideals and morals, one in purpose, and one in love.

St. Paul spoke of your oneness in love in these words: "Love seeks not its own. It is patient and understanding and is not easily provoked. Love does not gloat over the faults of the other, but affirms his or her good. Love is not judgmental, but forgives. It believes all things. Love never ends." (1 Corinthians 13:4-8a)

Even as you already in your engagement period were drawn together in communion with one another, even as you have experienced choosing and being chosen, even as you have already joined in sharing your deepest thoughts and ideals, even as you already are sharing with each other devotion and love, even so, it is God's will that you continue in this oneness . . . that you allow it to deepen and mature, always continuing to turn toward one another in understanding and intimacy, in happiness and sorrow, in common labor for the good of your home and family, as you experience joy and wonder, as you explore and grow in your personal relationships, as beings created by God. It is God's will that your turning toward each other, your harmony with each other in Spirit and in Body, be the foundation of your marriage, be the foundation of your home, be the foundation of whatever family you have.

In this oneness you will cherish each other, delight in each other, accept each other . . . the attributes of personality each one has, the character and ideals, and even imperfections . . . each one has. In this oneness may you never seek to grow apart through indifference, through preoccupation with lesser concerns, but always seek to be refreshed and enriched through God's will and his Word.

Sermonette

(To the altar) Groom: _______________ , do you choose me to be your husband? Will you love, respect, and honor me, sharing your plans and interests, ideals and emotions, through crisis and anxiety, through joy and pleasure, caring for me in lifelong commitment?

Bride: I will.

Bride: _______________ , do you choose me to be your wife? Will you love, respect, and honor me, sharing your plans and interests, ideals and emotions, through crisis and anxiety, through joy and pleasure, caring for me in lifelong commitment?

Groom: I will. I join you in marriage, _______________ , to know you as my wife, to share all of life with you, its responsibilities and freedoms, its tensions and trials, to cherish and care for you, and with you to follow God's leading. This I promise to you.

Bride: I join you in marriage, _______________ , to know you as my husband, to share all of life with you, its responsibilities and freedoms, its tensions and trials, to cherish and care for you, and with you to follow God's leading. This is my promise to you.

Now, therefore, in this spirit of loving oneness of which Christ speaks, may you strive to know one another in the biblical sense of knowing the whole person, body, mind, and spirit; of sharing, yet respecting each other as a self. As this paradox becomes true in your lives, this sharing of solitudes, this drawing together of male and female into a creative oneness, may your love blossom into a most blessed relationship, a blessing for each other, for whatever children you may have, and for the responsibilities you face together in God's world.

(Pastor receives rings — gives ring to Groom to place on Bride's finger.)

Groom: I give you, _______________ , this ring as a symbol of my love and faithfulness.

(Bride receives ring from pastor and repeats.)

Bride: I give you, _______________ , this ring as a symbol of my love and faithfulness.

(Light wedding candle.)

Because _______________ and _______________ have pledged their mutual love in marriage, declaring it before God and this gathering of his people, I pronounce them husband and wife in the name of the Father, Son, and Holy Spirit. Amen

(Couple kneel.) The Lord God who created our first parents and looked with favor on their union, bless you and make you holy, that in your whole beings you may please him, and that you may always live together in joy and love.

Heavenly Father, out of all the human family you have brought together these two persons and united them in marriage. Grant _______________ and _______________ the grace of faithfulness and true affection toward each other. May their love, in oneness, be patterned after that love which according to your Word, is slow to lose patience, looks for ways of being constructive, is not possessive, knows no limits to its endurance, no end to its trust, or fading of its hope. In good days and bad, strengthen and defend them. Keep their love for you and their fellowship with the church, creative and healthy, that the joys and blessings of this life may be a foretaste of the life to come, through Jesus Christ our Lord, in whose name he taught us to pray . . .

The Lord's Prayer (In unison)

Benediction

Couple Embrace

8

Unique characteristics in this ceremony:

In this service the meditation concerning marriage is a beautiful poem chosen by the bride and groom to be read as an expression of the feelings they share with each other.

The vows are contemporary, but the exchange of the rings uses traditional language. Before the declaration of marriage, there is a pastoral admonition to the couple. The declaration of marriage comes at the end after the prayers, but just before the benediction.

The marriage service of ______________ and ______________ on ______________ .

Invocation: In the name of the Father, and of the Son, and of the Holy Spirit. Amen

Greeting and Charge to Congregation: Dear friends, this gathering is a time of joy and gladness. You have been asked to share in the marriage of ______________ and ______________ . It signifies to them a stage in the process of becoming, of self-realization for each of them, and now for both together, one that began at an earlier time and will continue as each of them grows and their friendship deepens. It is for them a covenant of becoming and a continuing celebration of God's gift of love and life. Love is patient and kind; love is not jealous or boastful; it is not arrogant or rude. Love does not insist on its own way; it is not irritable or resentful; it does not rejoice at wrong, but rejoices in the right. Love bears all things, believes all things, hopes all things, endures all things. (1 Corinthians 13:4-8a)

Let us pray: Our Father, bless these as they come before family, friends, and church to affirm the choice that they have made of each other as life's partner. Grant them a seriousness of purpose that they may be delivered from empty words and casual commitments. For fulfilment of their vows, may they experience daily the love which only you can give. Through the love of Jesus Christ we pray. Amen

Engagement Vows and Approval: ______________ , will you take this woman as your wife; will you be faithful to her in love and honor, offering her encouragement and companionship; and will you live with her and cherish her in the bond of marriage?

Groom: I will.

_______________ , will you take this man as your husband, and will you honor and respect him, will you give him strength and encouragement, will you love him and faithfully cherish him in the bond of marriage?

Bride: I will.

Who gives this woman to marry this man?

Father: Her mother and father do.

(To altar)

Meditation Concerning Marriage: _______________ and _______________ have chosen these words to express the feelings they share for one another:

I love you,
Not only for what you are
But for what I am
When I am with you.
I love you
Not only for what
You have made of yourself
But for what
You are making of me.
I love you
For the part of me
That you bring out;
For putting your hand
Into my heaped-up heart
And passing over
All the foolish, weak things
That you can't help
Dimly seeing there,
And for drawing out
Into the light
All the beautiful belongings
That no one else had looked
Quite far enough to find.
I love you because you
Are helping me to make
Of the lumber of my life
Not a tavern
But a temple;
Out of works
Of my every day
Not a reproach
But a song.
I love you
Because you have done
More than any creed
Could have done
To make me good,
And more than any fate
Could have done
To make me happy.
You have done it
Without a touch,
Without a word,
Without a sign.
You have done it
By being yourself,
My companion and comforter,
Guide and friend.
The one I love.*

*From *Contemporary Worship Services*, by James L. Christensen, Copyright © 1971 by Fleming H. Revell Company. Used by permission.

Exchange of Wedding Vows: _____________ and _____________ , if it is your intention to share with each other all that the years will bring, by your promises bind yourselves now to each other as husband and wife.

Groom: _____________ , I take you to be my wife from this time onward,

to join with you and to share all that is to come,
to give and to receive,
to speak and to listen,
to inspire and to respond,
and in all circumstances of our life together
to be loyal to you with all my being.

Bride: _____________ , I take you to be my husband, from this time onward,

to join with you and to share all that is to come,
to give and to receive,
to speak and to listen,
to inspire and to respond,
and in all circumstances of our life together
to be loyal to you with all my being.

Exchange of Rings: (To Groom) _____________ , take this ring and place it on the wedding finger of _____________ and repeat, "With this ring, I thee wed." In the name of the Father, and of the Son, and of the Holy Spirit. Amen

(To Bride) _____________ , take this ring and place it on the wedding finger of _____________ and repeat, "With this ring, I thee wed." In the name of the Father, and of the Son, and of the Holy Spirit. Amen

(Kneel) The Lord God who created our first parents and sanctified their union in marriage sanctify and bless you, that you may please him both in body and soul, and live together in holy love until life's end. Amen

The Lord's Prayer

(Arise) Marriage requires much generosity, unselfishness, patience and love. The happiness of your marriage depends upon the inner experience of your heart and the strength of your commitment. If marriage is to be maintained at a high level for both of you, this commitment must be practiced daily. Two people are not married in the ceremony exclusively; you have only begun to be married. What is begun must continue with increased meaning throughout your life.

Declaration of Marriage: (Join right hands) ______________ and ______________ , since you have promised your love to each other, and before God and these witnesses have exchanged these solemn vows, as a minister of Jesus, I declare you to be husband and wife in the Name of the Father, and of the Son, and of the Holy Spirit. "What God has joined together, let no man put asunder."

Benediction: May the peace of God dwell in your hearts and in your home. May you have true friends to stand by you, both in joy and in sorrow. May you be strong in grace and love, now and forever. Amen

(Kiss the bride.)

9

Unique characteristics in this ceremony:

This service is relatively simple, incorporating all the parts of a traditional service. While omitting any Scripture lesson, the tone of the wedding service is, of course, biblically oriented. The ritual blends the exchanging of the vows, with the exchange of the rings and the declaration of marriage is at the end, just before the benediction.

The marriage service of ______________ and ______________ on ______________ .

Call to Worship: In the name of the Father, the Son, and the Holy Spirit. Amen (Congregation seated)

Tonight we have come to witness the marriage vows of ______________ and ______________ and to ask God's blessing upon their life together.

Invocation Prayer: Let us pray: O God, who alone unites persons in holy bonds of covenant, without whose Spirit there is no abiding unity, be present in the inner being of these who desire to be married and among these who have come to witness their commitment to each other in the Spirit of the Love of Christ. Amen

The Symbolic Approval: Who will, in behalf of the families and friends of ______________ and ______________ , give blessing upon this marriage? (We will — Mother and Father.)

The Meditation Concerning Marriage.

Declaration of Intention: Marriage has great possibility of success and failure as well as joy and pain. The possibility of sorrow and happiness is greater in married life than in single life. The person who has not made the wager of devotion cannot be hurt by another as can the person who puts his faith in another, nor can he know joy as the one, who shares all with a trusted, loving companion.

Are you ready in the presence of this community to declare your intention to this undertaking of faith and love?

(To Groom) ______________ , are you willing to receive ______________ as your wife, having full confidence that your abiding faith in each other will last a lifetime?

(Answer: I am.)

(To Bride) ______________ , are you willing to receive ______________ as your husband, having full confidence that your abiding faith in each other will last a lifetime?

(Answer: I am.)

(To the altar.)

Let us pray: Heavenly Father, who ordained marriage for your children, and gave us love, we present these two who wish to be married. May their union be blessed with true devotion, spiritual commitment and love. God, give these two the ability to keep the covenant made between them. When selfishness shows itself, grant generosity; when mistrust is a temptation, give moral strength; where there is a misunderstanding, give patience and gentleness. When suffering becomes their lot, give them a strong faith and abiding hope. Amen

The Exchange of Wedding Vows: Marriage requires much generosity, unselfishness, flexibility, patience and love from both husband and wife. Under it lies responsibility of home and community, but when supported by all the commitments of love, these responsibilities do not weigh heavily. The realness and happiness of your marriage depend upon the inner experience of your heart and the strength of your commitment.

Rings: As a symbol of your commitment you have chosen rings.

______________ , will you place this ring upon the finger of your bride and say your promise to her?

Groom: ______________ , I take you to be my wife from this time onward, to join with you and to share all that is to come, to give and to receive, to speak and to listen, to inspire and to respond, and in all circumstances of our life together, to be loyal to you with my whole life and with all my being so that together we may serve God and others as long as we both shall live.

Bride: ______________ , I take you to be my husband from this time onward, to join with you and to share all that is to come, to give and to receive, to speak and to listen, to inspire and to respond, and in all circumstances of our life together, to be loyal to you with my whole life and with all my being so that together we may serve God and others as long as we both shall live.

Candle: Symbolic of the fact that your lives have become one.

Charge to the Couple: If marriage is to be maintained at a high level for both of you, this commitment must be practiced daily. Two people are not married in the ceremony; you only begin to be married. What is begun must continue with increasing meaning.

The trials which married life encounters are great; only a strong commitment and spiritual motivations can maintain it. Mere physical attractiveness is not enough. Only the love of God will suffice.

(Kneel) The Lord God who created our first parents and sanctified their union in marriage; sanctify and bless you, that you may please him both in body and soul, and live together in Holy Love until life's end. Amen

The Lord's Prayer (In unison).

The Declaration of Marriage: (Join your right hands.) _______________ and _______________ , since you have consented together to be married and have witnessed the same before God and this community of relatives and friends and have committed love and faith to each other and have sealed the promises with rings, I announce that God has made you husband and wife, in the name of the Father, and the Son, and the Holy Spirit.

Benediction: May the Father, Son and Holy Spirit direct and keep you in truth and love all the days of your life. Amen

You may kiss the bride.

10

Unique characteristics in this ceremony:

This ceremony is built around the meaning of love. After listening to words about love in 1 John, the couple shares what love means to them.

Between the exchange of rings and vows, there is a prayer for God's guidance and love. There is a charge to the couple following the exchange of rings and vows, stressing the truth that marriage is a process.

The marriage service of ____________ and ____________ on ____________ .

Call to Worship: In the name of the Father, the Son, and the Holy Spirit. Amen (Congregation seated)

Today we have come to witness the marriage vows of ____________ and ____________ and to ask God's blessing on their life together.

Invocation Prayer: Let us pray: O God, who alone unites persons in Holy bonds of covenant, without whose spirit there is no abiding unity, be present in the inner being of these who have come to witness their commitment to each other — in the Spirit of the Love of Christ. Amen

Meditation Concerning Marriage: A wedding is the celebration of the highest we know in love, the pledging of two lives to common goals.

____________ and ____________ , as you think about making your vows to each other, realize that your destinies will be woven together in such a pattern that sorrow for one will be sorrow for the other and joy for one will be joy for the other. Today you commit yourselves to each other to give support and love in all times. The words "I love you," first spoken shyly in months gone by, are now spoken in full commitment of yourselves to each other. This love you share is God's gift. We love because he first loved us. This is expressed in the New Testament in the First Letter of John:

> "Friends, let us practice loving each other, for love comes from God and those who are loving and kind show that they

are the children of God, and that they are getting to know him better. But if a person isn't loving and kind, it shows that he doesn't know God, for God is love.

"God showed how much he loved us by sending his only son into this world to bring us eternal life through his death. In this act we see what real love is. It's not our love for God, but his love for us when he sent his son to satisfy God's anger against our sins.

"Friends, since God loved us as much as that, we surely ought to love each other, too." (1 John 4:7-11)

_____________ and _____________ have found a way to publicly express their love for each other with words of this poem:

Love is a look, a smile, brief as an instant,
long as eternity, a spark engendered by a
reaching out, a touch of hands, an intuition
that knows how to heal a hurt, and how to build a world.

For love's sake only, cherishing each other,
lovers move freely within a circle, that
defines their being, shapes what they become,
and thus they are fulfilled each in the other.

When love speaks in feeling,
love responds in instant recognition,
in embrace and letting go, always in the certainty of renewal.
Shared sorrows, disappointments only serve to strengthen love.

Let this be a pledge of love's safekeeping,
that in sleep, lovers dream each other's self,
and when they wake in the morning, some new insight,
some lovely memory of the other,
warms and draws and holds them close together.

So love begins in longing,
Love is transformed into belonging.

The Charge to the Congregation: True marriage can never be private or secret because in its course it has a public character. Not only on their wedding day, but in its entire course, it has aspects which are public. The community has a stake in this union and deserves the joy of participation. The families involved come to give their blessing to this union. Today what happens at the altar is the sanction of the Christian community. The most important part happens, not at the altar, but when two people realize that fullness of life for them according to God's plan involves a complete unity of lives.

Let us pray: Our Father, bless these as they come before family, friends, and church to affirm the choice that they have made of each other as life's partner and their intention to establish a home where your love may be celebrated in the family. Grant them a seriousness of purpose that they may be delivered from empty words and casual commitments. For the fulfilment of their vows, may they experience daily the love which only you can give. May your word nurture them that their lives will be fulfilled by doing your will. As we share with them in the celebration of their love, may we all grow toward the perfection that is experienced in your love. Through the love of Jesus Christ we pray. Amen

Symbolic Approval: Who will, in behalf of the family and friends of ______________ and ______________ give their approval for this woman to be the wife of this man?

Father/Parents — "I will/We will."

(To altar.)

Declaration of Intention: Marriage has a great possibility of success and failure as well as pain and joy. The person who has not made the wager of devotion cannot be hurt by another as can the person who puts his faith in another, nor can he share in the joy and laughter as the one who shares all with a trusted, loving companion.

______________ and ______________ , if it is your intention to share with each other your laughter and your tears and all that the years will bring, by your promises bind yourselves now to each other as husband and wife.

Exchange of Wedding Vows: Groom: ______________ , I take you to be my wife from this time onward,

to join with you and share all that is to come
to give and receive,
to speak and to listen,
to inspire and to respond,
and in all circumstances of our life together
to be loyal to you with my whole life and with all my being
through the best and the worst of what is to come as long as we live.

Bride: ______________, I take you to be my husband from this time onward,

to join with you and share all that is to come
to give and receive,
to speak and to listen,
to inspire and to respond
and in all circumstances of our life together
to be loyal to you with my whole life
and with all my being
through the best and the worst of what is to come as long as we live.

Prayer: Heavenly Father, who ordained marriage for your children, and gave us love, we present these two who wish to be married. May their union be blessed with true devotion, spiritual commitment, and love. God, give these two the ability to keep the covenant made between them. When selfishness shows itself, grant generosity; when mistrust is a temptation, give moral strength; when there is a misunderstanding, give patience and gentleness. When suffering becomes their lot, give them a strong faith and abiding hope. Amen

Exchange of Rings: Marriage requires much generosity, unselfishness, flexibility, patience, and love. Under it lies responsibility of home and community, but when supported by all the commitments of love, this responsibility does not weigh heavily. The realness and happiness of your marriage depends upon the inner experience of your heart and the strength of your commitment. As a symbol of commitment you have chosen rings.

(To Groom) ______________, take this ring and place it on the wedding finger of ______________ and repeat: "With this ring, I thee wed. In the name of the Father, and of the Son, and of the Holy Spirit. Amen"

(To Bride ______________, take this ring and place it on the wedding finger of ______________ and repeat: "With this ring, I thee wed. In the name of the Father, and of the Son, and of the Holy Spirit. Amen"

Charge to the Couple: If marriage is to be maintained at a high level for both of you, this commitment must be practiced daily. Two people are not married in the ceremony exclusively; you only have begun to be married. What is begun must continue with increased meaning. Throughout your marriage, may you have enough tears to be sensitive, enough hurt to be human, enough pride to feel pain, and enough selfishness to need love.

The Blessing: (Kneel) The Lord God, who created our first parents and established them in marriage, establish and sustain you that you may find delight in each other and grow in holy love until your life's end. May you dwell in God's presence forever; may true and constant love preserve you.

The Declaration of Marriage: ______________ and ______________ , since you have promised your love to each other, and before God and these witnesses have exchanged these solemn vows and these symbols of undying love, as a minister of the gospel of Jesus Christ, I now pronounce you man and wife. "What therefore God has joined together, let no man put asunder."

The Benediction: May the Father, Son, and Holy Spirit direct and keep you in truth and love all the days of your life. Amen

Kiss the Bride.

11

Unique characteristics in this ceremony:

There is nothing new in this service, except the ability of taking various parts of several other ceremonies and fitting them together in a meaningful and traditional way.

Included in the vows is a promise that the bride and groom will respect each other as individuals. When the time comes for lighting the unity candle, they take the two side candles and light the large wedding candle, but then leave the two small side candles burning: they remain individuals even while becoming one in marriage.

The marriage service of ______________ and ______________ on ______________ .

Call to Worship: In the name of the Father, the Son, and the Holy Spirit. Amen

On this occasion ______________ and ______________ come before family, friends and church to affirm the choice that they have made of each other as life companions.

Invocation Prayer: Let us pray: O God, who alone unites persons in holy bonds of covenant, without whose Spirit there is no abiding unity. Be present in the inner being of these who desire to be married and among these who have come to witness their commitment to each other. In the Spirit of the love of Christ. Amen (Congregation seated.)

Symbolic Approval: Who will in behalf of the families and friends of ______________ and ______________ give blessing upon this marriage?

Father: "I do."

Meditation Concerning Marriage: A wedding is the celebration of the highest we know in love, the pledging of two lives to common goals. ______________ and ______________ , as you think about making your vows to each other, realize that your destinies will be woven together in such a pattern that sorrow for one will be sorrow for the other and joy for one will be joy for the other. Today you commit yourselves to each other to give support and love in all times.

The words "I love you" first spoken shyly in months gone by are now spoken in full commitment of yourselves to each other. This love you share is God's gift. We love because he first loved us.

St. Paul writes: Love is patient and kind and envies no one. Love is never boastful, nor conceited, nor rude, never selfish, not quick to offense. Love keeps no score of wrongs, does not gloat over other men's sins, but delights in truth. There is nothing love cannot face; there is no limit to its faith, its hope and its endurance. Love will never come to an end.

To be loved is to know happiness and contentment, to give love is to know the joy of sharing oneself . . . for it is through the miracle of love that we discover the fullness of life.

Declaration of Intention: Marriage has great possibility of success and failure as well as joy and pain. The possibility of sorrow and happiness is greater in married life than in single life. The person who has not made the wager of devotion cannot be hurt by another as can the person who puts his faith in another, nor can he know joy as the one who shares all with a trusted, loving companion.

Are you ready in the presence of this community to declare your intention to this undertaking of faith and love?

(To Groom) Are you willing to receive ______________ as your wife, having full confidence that your abiding faith in each other will last a lifetime?

Answer: "I am."

(To Bride) Are you willing to receive ______________ as your husband, having full confidence that your abiding faith in each other will last a lifetime?

Answer: "I am."

(To altar.)

Prayer: Let us pray: Heavenly Father, who ordained marriage for your children and gave us love, we present these two who wish to be married. May their union be blessed with true devotion, spiritual commitment and love. God, give these two the ability to keep the covenant made between them. When selfishness shows itself, grant generosity; when mistrust is a temptation, give moral strength; when there is a misunderstanding, give patience and gentleness. When suffering becomes their lot, give them a strong faith and abiding hope. Amen

Exchange of Wedding Vows: Groom: I, ______________ , having full confidence that our abiding faith in each other as human beings will last our lifetime, take you _______________, to be my wedded wife. I promise to be your loving and faithful husband in prosperity and in need, in joy and in sorrow, in sickness and in health, and to respect your privileges as an individual as long as we both shall live.

Bride: I, _______________, having full confidence that our abiding faith in each other as human beings will last our lifetime, take you _______________, to be my wedded husband. I promise to be your loving and faithful wife in prosperity and in need, in joy and in sorrow, in sickness and in health, and to respect your privileges as an individual as long as we both shall live.

Service of Rings: From the earliest time, the golden circle has been a symbol of wedded love. (Minister receives rings.) It is made of pure gold to symbolize pure love. Being one unbroken circle, it symbolizes unending love you promise.

(To Groom) Take this ring which you have selected, place it upon the finger of _______________ and say to her these words:

Groom: "This ring I give you, in token and pledge of my constant faith and abiding love."

(To Bride) Take this ring which you have selected, place it upon the finger of _______________ and say to him these words:

Bride: "This ring I give you, in token and pledge of my constant faith and abiding love."

Lighting of the Wedding Candle

Charge to the Couple: If marriage is to be maintained at a high level for both of you, this commitment must be practiced daily. Two people are not married in the ceremony; you only begin to be married. What is begun must continue with increasing meaning. The trials which married life encounters are great; only a strong commitment and spiritual motivation can maintain it. Mere physical attractiveness is not enough. Only the love of God will suffice.

(Kneel)

Prayer: The Lord God who created our first parents and sanctified their union in marriage: Sanctify and bless you that you may please him both in body and soul and live together in holy love until life's end. Amen

The Lord's Prayer (In unison)

(Rise)

Declaration of Marriage: (Join right hands.) _______________ and _______________, since you have consented together to be married and have witnessed the same before God and this community of relatives and friends and have committed love and faith to each other and have sealed the promises with rings, I announce that God has made you husband and wife, in the name of the Father, and the Son, and the Holy Spirit.

Benediction: May the Father, Son and Holy Spirit direct and keep you in trust and love all the days of your life. Amen

Kiss the Bride.

12

Unique characteristics of this ceremony:

Performed out of doors, the flowery language of Kahil Gibran with its symbolism from nature is appropriate. The groom's vows are expanded to include the feelings and sentiments of both bride and groom. The couple chose to combine the vows with the giving and receiving of the rings.

The service concludes with another writing from Gibran, emphasizing the freedom each has exercised in choosing a life's mate and the individuality which must continue in the marriage.

The marriage service of ______________ and ______________ on ______________ .

Invocation: In the name of the Father, the Son, and the Holy Spirit. Amen

On this occasion ______________ and ______________ come before family, friends, and church to affirm the choice that they have made of each other as life's mate and their intention to establish a home for the raising of a family and the fulfilment of life together.

As the years go by, you will realize that this marriage you have chosen for yourselves was not given to you by anyone else. It has been, and must continue to be, a process that builds throughout your lives. You must work at it day by day, meeting the disappointments, as well as the joys, that your lives together will bring. We have gathered with you this evening to help you give added life to this marriage that you have chosen for yourselves. But, in doing this, we realize that this outward act is but a symbol of that which is inward and real, a union of two people, which a church may bless and the state may make legal, but which neither church nor state can create or annul. It is such a union, by your own free choice — and with full knowledge of what that choice means — that you two have come to live.

From *The Prophet.* Let us pray:

> "When you love you should not say, 'God is in my heart,' but rather, 'I am in the heart of God.' And think not you can direct the course of love, for love, if it finds you worthy, directs your course. Love has no other desire but to fulfill itself. But if you

love and must needs have desires, let these be your desires: To melt and be like a running brook that sings its melody to the night. To know the pain of too much tenderness. To be wounded by your own understanding of love; And to bleed willingly and joyfully. To wake at dawn with a winged heart and give thanks for another day of loving; To rest at the noon hour and meditate love's ecstasy; To return home at eventide with gratitude; And then to sleep with a prayer for the beloved in your heart and a song of praise upon your lips."*

Are you now ready in the presence of family and friends to declare your intention to make this venture of faith and love?

(To Groom) ______________ , are you willing to receive ______________ as your wife, having full confidence that your abiding faith in each other as human beings will last forever?

Answer: "I am."

(To Bride) ______________ , are you willing to receive ______________ as your husband, having full confidence that your abiding faith in each other as human beings will last forever?

Answer: "I am."

Now who will, in behalf of their families and friends proclaim that ______________ and ______________ should be united as husband and wife?

Families answer: "We do."

(To altar.)

Prayer: Let us pray: Heavenly Father, who has endowed us with creative ability in love, we present to you these who have disclosed their wish to be married. May their union be endowed with true devotion, spiritual commitment, and personal integrity. O God, give to this woman, ______________ , and to this man, ______________ , the ability to keep the bond between them made. When selfishness shows itself, grant generosity; when mistrust is a temptation, give moral strength; where misunderstanding intrudes, give patience and gentleness. When suffering becomes their lot, give them a strong faith and abiding hope. Amen

Marriage requires much of generosity, unselfishness, flexibility and forbearance from both husband and wife. The reality and happiness of your marriage depends upon the inner experience of your heart and the integrity of your commitment.

*Reprinted from *The Prophet*, by Kahlil Gibran, by permission of Alfred A. Knopf, Inc.

Rings: As a seal of your promise, you each have chosen rings of precious metal, symbolizing the unity, wholeness and endlessness of your life together. Will you, ______________, place this ring upon the wedding finger of your bride and say your promise to her?

Groom: I, ______________, take you, ______________, to be the wife of my days,
To be the mother of our children, to be the companion of my home.
I will leave all and come and make the hymns of you,
None has understood you, but I understand you,
None has done justice to you, you have not done justice to yourself,
Others have found you imperfect, I only find no imperfection in you,
Others would subordinate you, I only am he who will never consent to subordinate you,
I only am he who places over you no master, owner, better, God, beyond what waits intrinsically in yourself.
We are, simple, spontaneous, curious,
Two souls interchanging
With the original testimony for us continued to the last.

Take this ring, freely, as a token of my love and as a symbol of my intention to live with you in love and respect. As this ring has no end, neither shall my love for you.

Will you, ______________, place this ring upon the wedded finger of your husband and say your promise to him?

Bride: I, ______________, take you, ______________, to be the husband of my days,
To be the father of our children, to be the companion of my home.
We shall keep together what share of sorrow our lives may lay upon us,
And we shall hold together our store of goodness and of love.

Take this ring, freely, as a token of my love and as a symbol of my intention to live with you in love and respect. As this ring has no end, neither shall my love for you.

Light Wedding Candle

From The Prophet comes a passage which serves to enlighten all of us as to the essence of the love which ______________ and

______________ have here professed:

"Love one another, but make not a bond of love: Let it rather be a moving sea between the shores of your souls. Fill each other's cup but drink not from one cup. Give one another of your bread but eat not from the same loaf. Sing and dance together and be joyous, but let each one of you be alone, Even as the strings of a lute are alone though they quiver with the same music. Give your hearts, but not into each other's keeping. For only the hand of Life can contain your hearts. And stand together yet not too near together: For the pillars of the temple stand apart, and the oak tree and the cypress grow not in each other's shadow."

(Kneel) Since you, ______________ and ______________, have consented together to be married and have witnessed the same before God and this community of relatives and friends, and have committed love to and faith in each other and have sealed the promises with rings, I announce that God has made you husband and wife.

Benediction

13

Unique characteristics in this ceremony:

There are some rather unique aspects in this service. Recognizing the wedding is a worship experience, the congregation is invited to join with the couple in worship. The couple also wishes to have the parents included more than is customary. The parents of both the bride and groom are asked for their consent and blessing upon the marriage. Roses are presented to the parents by the bride and groom early in the ceremony rather than at the end.

The marriage service of ______________ **and** ______________ **on** ______________ .

Invocation: In the name of the Father, and of the Son, and of the Holy Spirit. Amen (Congregation seated)

My friends, you have been invited to this wedding service not in order for you to observe it, but rather because ______________ and ______________ have asked you to share in it with them. For above all, this is a service of worship, which means we are here not to honor ______________ and ______________ , but rather to give praise to God. For God is the source of all true love, including that which now binds ______________ and ______________ to each other. Specifically, therefore, we are here to celebrate and share in a glorious act that God is about to perform — the act by which he converts the love which ______________ and ______________ have for each other into the holy and sacred estate of marriage.

Scripture Reading: (1 John 4:7-12) Beloved, let us love one another; for love is of God and he who loves is born of God and knows God. He who does not love does not know God, for God is love. In this the love of God was made manifest among us, that God sent his only Son into the world, so that we might live through him. In this is love, not that we loved God but that he loves us and sent his Son to be the expiation for our sins. Beloved, if God so loves us, we also ought to love one another. No man has ever seen God; if we love one another, God abides in us and his love is perfected in us.

The Celebration of Marriage: Do you ______________ and

______________ agree that your daughter, ______________ , should now be united in marriage with ______________ ?

Answer: "We do."

Do you ______________ and ______________ agree that your son, ______________ , should now be united in marriage with ______________ ?

Answer: "We do."

In light of these words signifying the blessing of your respective families, I ask you, ______________ and ______________ , to come to the altar and participate in the celebration for marriage by the exchanging of vows and the giving of rings.

(To altar.)

Presentation of Roses to Parents: ______________ and ______________ ask you ______________ and ______________ to take these roses in token of their gratitude and their love and know that they too rejoice in their new adult relationship with you. (Present roses to parents.)

Charge to the Couple: ______________ and ______________ , it is absolutely essential that you realize the enormity of what you are about to undertake with these vows. Because you are human and therefore subject to error and temptation as all humans are, and because you have no idea what the future holds for you — what joys and what sorrows await you, your decision to marry requires tremendous faith on each of your parts. You must have faith in yourselves as individuals and in what you have to give each other, faith in your relationship as a couple, and in what you can be and do together, and most of all, faith in God and in his presence with you to face whatever the future holds. You must never forget that the marriage vows are not just vows of love — but, they are vows of faithful love for each other grounded in God's love for you both.

Vows: Face each other and repeat after me:

Groom: I, ______________ , do take you, ______________ , to be my lawful wedded wife, and trusting in God's help, I promise to faithfully love you, for better for worse, for richer for poorer, in sickness and in health. I will love you, and honor you, as long as we both shall live.

Bride: I, ______________ , do take you, ______________ , to be my lawful wedded husband, and trusting in God's help, I promise to faithfully love you, for better for worse, for richer for poorer, in sickness and in health. I will love you, and honor you, as long as we both shall live.

Rings: From the earliest time, the golden circle has been a symbol of wedded love. (Minister receives rings.) It is made of pure gold to symbolize pure love. Being one unbroken circle, it symbolizes the unending love you promise.

(To Groom) ______________ , take this ring which you have selected, place it upon the finger of ______________ , and say to her these words:

"With this ring I thee wed, in the name of the Father, and of the Son, and of the Holy Spirit."

(To Bride) ______________ , take this ring which you have selected, place it upon the finger of ______________ , and say to him these words:

"With this ring I thee wed, in the name of the Father, and of the Son, and of the Holy Spirit."

Candle Lighting: Symbolic of two lives now becoming one.

"It is not good that the man should be alone . . . Therefore a man leaves his father and his mother, and cleaves to his wife, and they become one flesh." (Genesis 2:18, 24)

As two lights are now blended into one, so two lives are blended into one. May you be one in name, one in aim, and one in happy destiny together.

(Kneel)

Prayer: Let us pray: The Lord God who created our first parents and sanctified their union in marriage, sanctify and bless you that you may please him both in body and soul and live together in holy love until life's end. Amen

The Lord's Prayer (In unison)

Declaration of Marriage: ______________ and ______________ have declared before God and before you, the members and friends of this congregation, that they will live together in marriage; they have made sacred promises to each other and they have symbolized those promises by joining hands and by exchanging rings, I therefore, pronounce them to be husband and wife together, in the name of the Father, the Son, and the Holy Spirit. What God has joined together, man must not separate.

Benediction: The Lord bless you and keep you,

The Lord make his face shine upon you and be gracious unto you.

The Lord lift up his countenance upon you and give you peace.

In the name of the Father, and of the Son, and of the Holy Spirit. Amen
You may kiss the bride.
I present Mr. and Mrs. ______________ ______________!

14

Unique characteristics in this ceremony:

In this service, the meditation concerning marriage is the beginning of pastoral statements to the couple which are inserted before the reading of the lesson from 1 John, and following the statement from Kahlil Gibran. There is another pastoral statement before the declaration of intention, another before the exchange of vows and rings which are one in this service, and another following the exchange of vows and rings.

The benediction asks that God will keep this couple in the love and truth expressed in the service all the days of their lives.

The marriage service of ______________ and ______________ on ______________ .

Call to Worship: In the name of the Father, and of the Son, and of the Holy Spirit. Amen

Tonight we have come to witness the marriage vows of ______________ and ______________ and to ask God's blessing upon their life together.

Invocation Prayer: O God, who alone unites persons in holy bonds of covenant, without whose Spirit there is no abiding unity; be present in the inner being of those who desire to be married and among these who have come to witness their commitment to each other — in the Spirit of the love of Christ. Amen

The Meditation Concerning Marriage: The occasion that declares publicly the intention of a man and a woman to enter into a marriage has become known in our society as a wedding. For the Christian, this occasion is not spectacle, but worship; it is not a mere formal observance, but a participation in the will of God for life; it is not just for ______________ and ______________ but for those of you who love to rededicate your love to your loved one. A wedding is the celebration of the highest we know in life — the pledging of two lives to common goals. A relationship so sacred and meaningful must be entered into thoughtfully and deliberately, not casually or thoughtlessly.

_______________ and _______________ , as you think about making your vows to each other, realize that your destinies will be woven of one design in such a pattern that sorrow for one will be sorrow for the other and joy for one will be joy for the other. Tonight you commit yourselves to each other to give support and love in all times. Listen to each other, share with each other and pray together. The words "I love you," first spoken shyly in months gone by, when it was not known if they would be accepted or returned in kind, are today spoken in the full commitment of yourselves to each other. This love you share is God's gift. We love because he first loved us. This is expressed in the New Testament in the Book of 1 John:

> "Friends, let us practice loving each other for love comes from God and those who are loving and kind show that they are the children of God and that they are getting to know him better. But if a person isn't loving and kind, it shows that he doesn't know God — for God is love.
>
> "God showed how much he loved us by sending his only Son into this world to bring us eternal life through his death. In this act we see what real love is; it's not our love for God, but his love for us when he sent his Son to satisfy God's anger against our sins.
>
> "Friends, since God loved us as much as that, we surely ought to love each other, too." (1 John 4:7-11)

God has shown us that love is an essential relationship. This gift from him is our joy.

Kahlil Gibran in his book *The Prophet* reflects on marriage. He says:

> Love one another, but make not a bond of love; Let it rather be a moving sea between the shores of your souls. Fill each other's cup but drink not from one cup. Give one another of your bread but eat not from the same loaf. Sing and dance together and be joyous, but let each one of you be alone. Even as the strings of a lute are alone though they quiver with the same music.

When two people marry, they bring with them all their experiences of their pasts. Each has strengths and knowledge to share with the other. Each is unique and thus their particular marriage will be unique. Each partner must respect the other's individualism. More than likely this individualism is what attracted each to the other.*

*Reprinted from *The Prophet*, by Kahlil Gibran, by permission of Alfred A. Knopf, Inc.

The Charge to the Congregation: True marriage can never be private or secret, because in its course it has a public character. Not only on their wedding day, but in its entire course, it has aspects which are public. The community has a stake in this union and deserves the joy of participation. The families involved come to give their blessing to this union. Tonight what happens at the altar is the sanction of the Christian Community. The most important part happens, not at the altar, but when two people realize that fullness of life for them according to God's plan involves a complete unity of lives.

Let us pray:

Our Father, bless these as they come before family, friends and church to affirm the choice that they have made of each other as a life's partner and their intention to establish a home where your love may be celebrated in the family. Grant them a seriousness of purpose that they may be delivered from empty words and casual commitments. For the fulfilment of their vows, may they experience daily the love which only you can give. May your word nurture them that their lives will be fulfiled by doing your will. As we share with them in the celebration of their love, may we all grow toward the perfection that is experienced in your love. Through the love of Jesus Christ we pray. Amen

The Symbolic Approval:

Who will, on behalf of the families and friends of ______________ and ______________ , give their blessing upon this marriage?

Father: I will

The Declaration of Intention:

Marriage has great possibility of success and failure as well asa joy and pain. The possibility of sorrow and happiness is greater in married life than in single life. The person who has not made the wager of devotion cannot be hurt by another as can the person who puts his faith in another, nor can he know the joy as the one who shares all with a trusted, loving companion.

Are you ready in the presence of this community to declare your intention to this undertaking of faith and love?

(To Groom:) ______________ , are you willing to receive ______________ as your wife, having full confidence that your abiding faith in each other will last a life time?

Answer: I am

(To Bride:) ______________ , are you willing to receive ______________ as your husband, having full confidence that your abiding faith in each other will last a life time?

Answer: I am

Prayer:

Heavenly Father, who ordained marriage for your children and gave us love, we present these two who wish to be married. May their union be blessed with true devotion, spiritual commitment and love. God, give these two the ability to keep the covenant made between them. When selfishness shows itself, grant generosity; when mistrust is a temptation, give moral strength; where there is a misunderstanding, give patience and gentleness. When suffering becomes their lot, give them a strong faith and abiding hope. Amen

(To altar)

The Exchange of Wedding Vows:

Marriage requires much generosity, unselfishness, flexibility, patience, and love from both husband and wife. Under it lies responsibility of home and community, but when supported by all the commitments of love, this responsibility does not weigh helvily. The realness and happiness of your marriage depends upon the inner experience of your heart and the strength of your commitment.

As a symbol of commitment, you have chosen rings. (Minister takes ring to groom) Will you place this ring upon the finger of your bride and say your promise to her?

Groom: In the presence of the Lord and before these friends I, ______________, take you ______________ to be my wife, promising with Christ's Spirit, to be your loving and faithful husband, in prosperity and in need, in joy and in sorrow, in sickness and in health, to honor and cherish you and respect your privileges as an individual as long as we both shall live. As this ring has no end, neither shall my love for you.

(Minister to Bride)

Will you place this ring upon the finger of your groom and say your promise to him?

Bride: In the presence of the Lord and before these friends I, ______________, take you ______________ to be my husband, promising with Christ's Spirit, to be your loving and faithful wife, in prosperity and in need, in joy and in sorrow, in sickness and in health, to honor and cherish you, to respect your individualism and to give you encouragement as long as we both shall live. As this ring has no end, neither shall my love for you.

Charge to the Couple:

If marriage is to be maintained at a high level for both of you, this commitment must be practiced daily. Two people are not married in the ceremony; you only begin to be married. What is begun must continue with increasing meaning.

The trials which married life encounters are great; only a strong commitment and spiritual motivation can maintain it. Mere physical attractiveness is not enough. Only the love of God will suffice.

The Lord's Prayer: (In unison)

The Declaration of Marriage:

______________ and ______________ , since you have consented together to be married and have witnessed the same before God and this community of relatives and friends and have committed love to and faith in each other and have sealed the promises with rings, I announce that God has made you husband and wife. In the name of the Father, and of the Son, and the Holy Spirit. Amen

The Benediction:

May the Father, Son and Holy Spirit direct and keep you in truth and love all the days of your life. Amen

15

Unique characteristics in this ceremony:

This service begins with scripture lessons from Genesis and 1 Corinthians before any other statement is made concerning the occasion of the wedding service. First we listen to God, and then we reflect upon what we are doing at this existential moment.

The vows are intimate, anticipating the crossing of the threshhold into married love and parenthood.

The Marriage Service of ____________ and ____________ on ____________

Invocation

In the name of the Father, and of the Son, and of the Holy Spirit. Amen

"It is not good that the man should be alone" (Genesis 2:18)

"Therefore a man leaves his father and his mother, and cleaves to his wife; and they become one flesh" (Genesis 2:24)

The quality of love for all of life's relationships has been described by the Apostle Paul in his unforgettable words from his first letter to the Corinthians, Chapter 13: "I may speak in tongues of men or of angels, but if I am without love, I am a sounding gong or a clanging cymbal. I may have the gift of prophecy, and know every hidden truth; I may have faith strong enough to move mountains; but if I have no love, I am nothing. I may dole out all I possess, or even give my body to be burnt, but if I have no love, I am none the better.

Love is patient; love is kind and envies no one. Love is never boastful, nor conceited, nor rude; never selfish, not quick to take offence. Love keeps no score of wrongs; does not gloat over other sins, but delights in the truth. There is nothing love cannot face; there is no limit to its faith, its hope, and its endurance.(1 Corinthians 13:1-7)

The Charge to the Congregation and the Couple:

On this occasion, ____________ and ____________ come before family, friends, and church to affirm the choice that they have made of each other as life's mates. They are declaring their intention to establish a home for the raising of a family and the fulfilment of life together. How like the church in its relationship to its Lord is the wedding of two people. May you see in this relationship of Christ and his Church the pattern of love and devotion for husband and wife.

(To Groom): ______________ , will you take this woman as your wife, will you be faithful to her in tender love and honor, offering her encouragement and companionship; and will you live with her, and cherish her, as love and respect would lead you, in the bond of marriage?

Answer: "I will"

(To Bride): ______________ , will you take this man as your husband and will you honor and respect him; will you give him strength and encouragement; will you love him and live with him as a mate, a companion, and a lover; and will you faithfully cherish him in the bonds of marriage?

Answer: "I will"

Who gives this woman to marry this man?

Father of the bride answers: "Her mother and father do."

Meditation:

______________ and ______________ , as you contemplate the making of your vows to each other, realize that henceforth your destinies shall be woven of one design and your perils and your joys shall not be known apart. Today you are making public, for all to know, that the words "I Love You" are a full commitment of yourselves to each other, to the forsaking of all other lovers, and to assuming of adult responsibility in society. Marriage has possibilities of failure and success as well as pain and joy, sorrow and happiness. The possibilities are greater in married life than in a single life. You have declared your intention to make this venture of faith and love.

Sermonette:

(To altar)

The Exchange of Wedding Vows:

Groom: Here before God, family and friends, I ______________ , do promise to share my hopes, dreams, and tears in marriage. I offer my heart when you are sorrowed, my hands when you are troubled and laughter when you are happy. I love you for the mother you will be and for being my best friend for now and forever. I will be faithful to you, honor you, and with guidance from God, I give you my name; I love you; I am your husband.

Bride: Here before God, family and friends, I ______________,
do promise to share my hopes, dreams and tears in marriage. I offer my heart when you are sorrowed, my hands when you are troubled, and laughter when you are happy. I love you for the father you will be and for being my best friend for now and forever. I will be faithful to you, honor you, and with guidance from God; I take your name; I love you; I am your wife.

The Service of Rings:

Bride and Groom: (As they exchange rings, in turn recite)

"As this ring has no end neither shall my love for you."

Lighting the Candle:

Symbolic of two lives becoming one.

The Wedding Prayer:

The Lord God who created our first parents and sanctified their union in marriage sanctify and bless you that you may please him both in body and soul and live together in holy love until life's end. Amen

Let us pray:

Eternal God, the spring of life and giver of spiritual grace, bless these our friends, that living together, they may fulfill the vows and covenant made between them. May they ever remain in perfect love and peace together according to your Spirit in Jesus Christ, our Lord. Amen

The Lord's Prayer:

The Benediction:

May the joy and peace which only God can give and which cannot be taken away by anything in this world, be yours today and in all of life's tomorrows. Amen

16

Unique characteristics in this ceremony:

This service uses as its first lesson, the Genesis story of the creation of man followed with Jesus' commandment to love one another from the fifteenth chapter of John.

After the sermonette, roses are presented to the parents, and the couple speak words of gratitude to them for what they have meant as Father and Mother

The statement of God concerning marriage from Mark 10 is said following the exchange of wedding vows. There is also included a blessing of the rings, symbols of love and fidelity.

The statement at the lighting of the unity candle speaks of the mental, spiritual, and physical bond that marriage brings to the couple in love.

The Marriage Service of ______________ and ______________ on ______________

Invocation:

In the name of the Father, and of the Son, and of the Holy Spirit. Amen

Let us pray;

O God, who alone united persons in the holy bonds of matrimony, without whose Spirit there is no abiding unity or oneness, be present with ______________ and ______________ and all who have come this evening to witness their commitment to each other in the Spirit of the love of Christ. Amen

Who will, in behalf of the families and friends of ______________ and ______________ , give blessings upon this marriage?

Father of Bride responds: Her mother and I do.

A wedding is the celebration of the highest we know in love, the pledging of two lives as one. ______________ and ______________ , as you think about making your vows to each other, realize that your destinies will be woven together in such a pattern that sorrow for one will be sorrow for the other and joy for one will be joy for the other. This evening you commit yourselves to each other to give support and love in all times. The words "I love you," first spoken shyly in months gone by, are now spoken in full commitment of yourselves to each other. This love you share is God's gift. We love because he first loved us.

First Reading: Genesis 1:26-31a

God said, "Let us make man in our own image, in the likeness of ourselves, and let them be masters of the fish of the sea, the birds of heaven, the cattle, all the wild beasts and all the reptiles that crawl upon the earth." God created man in the image of himself, in the image of God he created him; male and female he created them.

God blessed them saying to them, "Be fruitful, multiply, fill the earth and conquer it. Be masters of the fish, the birds of heaven and all living animals on the earth." God saw all he had made, and indeed it was very good.

Second Reading: John 15:12-16

Jesus said to his disciples:

"This is my commandment; love one another as I have loved you. A man can have no greater love than to lay down his life for his friends. You are my friends, if you do what I command you" —

Sermonette:

Thank Parents: Couple gives roses to parents.

(To altar)

Wedding Vows: Join right hands

Groom: I ______________ , take you, ______________ , to be my wife. I promise to be true to you in good times and in bad times, in sickness and in health. I will love you and honor you all the days of my life.

Bride: I, ______________ , take you, ______________ , to be my husband. I promise to be true to you in good times and in bad times, in sickness and in health. I will love you and honor you all the days of my life.

What God has joined, men must not divide. Amen

Rings:

May the Lord bless these rings which you give to each other as a sign of your love and fidelity. Amen

(To Groom): ______________, take this ring as a sign of my love and fidelity. In the name of the Father, and of the Son, and of the Holy Spirit.

(To Bride): ______________ , take this ring as a sign of my love and fidelity. In the name of the Father, and of the Son, and of the Holy

Spirit.

Light Wedding Candle: Symbolic of fact, your lives have now become one.

Love is the most powerful force in the universe. Not time, birth, death or rebirth can finally separate those who have formed a deep mental, spiritual or physical bond. The soul's affinity has been established, and those who know or have known love will always be "one."

(Kneel)

Prayers:

The Lord God who created our first parents and sanctified their union in marriage, sanctify and bless you that you may please him both in body and soul and live together in holy love until life's end. Amen

The Lord's Prayer: (in unison)

(Join right hands)

_______________ and _______________ , since you have consented together to be married and have witnessed the same before God and this community of relatives and friends and have commited love and faith to each other and have sealed promises with rings, I announce that God has made you husband and wife. In the name of the Father, and of the Son, and of the Holy Spirit.

May the Father, Son and Holy Spirit direct and keep you in trust and love all the days of your lives. Amen

Kiss the Bride

It is my privilege to introduce to you Mr. and Mrs. _______________ _______________ !!

17

Unique characteristics in this ceremony:

At the beginning of this service, the bride and groom dedicate a song in loving thankfulness to their parents. There are five readings from Scripture in this service and a meditation which uses the lessons to explain love and marriage.

The statement of intention contains elements more conventionally found in the marriage vows, and the exchange of rings is joined with the vows into one act.

Following the exchange of vows and rings and the lighting of the unity candle, the words of Kahlil Gibran are read as the profession of the couple's love for one another, and the charge to the couple comes just before the Lord's Prayer and declaration of marriage.

The marriage service of ______________ and ______________ on ______________ .

Call to Worship: In the name of the Father, and of the Son, and of the Holy Spirit. Amen

Tonight we have come to witness the marriage vows of ______________ and ______________ and to ask God's blessing upon their life together.

Invocation Prayer: O God, who alone unites persons in holy bonds of covenant, without whose Spirit there is no abiding unity. Be present in the inner being of these who desire to be married this day and among these who have come to witness their commitment to each other. In the Spirit of the Love of Christ. Amen

Symbolic Approval: Who will, in behalf of the families and friends of ______________ and ______________ , give their blessing upon this marriage? (Mother and Father respond.)

As ______________ and ______________ begin their new life together today, they would like to dedicate this song in loving thankfulness to their parents.

Scripture Lessons: Listen to what the Word of God teaches concerning marriage.

The Lord God said: "It is not good that the man should be alone; I will make a helper fit for him." (Genesis 2:18)

Our Lord Jesus Christ said: "From the beginning of creation, God made them male and female. And for this reason a man shall leave his father and mother and be joined to his wife, and the two shall become one. So they are no longer two but one. What therefore God has joined together, let not man put asunder. (Mark 10:6-9)

The Apostle Paul, speaking by the Holy Spirit says this about love: "Love is patient and kind; love is not jealous or boastful; it is not arrogant or rude. Love does not insist on its own way; it is not irritable or resentful; it does not rejoice at wrong, but rejoices in the right. Love bears all things, hopes all things, endures all things. Love never fails." (1 Corinthians 13:4-8)

In the First Letter of St. John we read: "Beloved, let us love one another; for love is of God, and he who loves is born of God and knows God. He who does not love does not know God; for God is love. In this the love of God was made manifest among us, that God sent his only Son into the world, so that we might live through him. In this is love, not that we loved God but that he loved us and sent his Son to be the expiation for our sins. Beloved, if God so loved us, we also ought to love one another. No man has ever seen God; but if we love one another, God abides in us, and his love is perfected in us. (1 John 4:7-12)

Song of Solomon 2:10-13, The Bride speaks: "My beloved answered, he said to me: Rise up, my darling; my fairest, come away. For now the winter is past, the rains are over and gone; the flowers appear in the country-side; the time is coming when the birds will sing, and the turtle-dove's cooing will be heard in our land; when the green figs will ripen on the fig-trees and the vines give forth their fragrance. Rise up, my darling; my fairest, come away."

And the Bridegroom responds: "Wear me as a seal upon your heart, as a seal upon your arm; for love is strong as death, passion cruel as the grave; it blazes up like blazing fire, fiercer than any flame. Many waters cannot quench love, no flood can sweep it away; if a man were to offer for love the whole wealth of his house, it would be utterly scorned."

The Meditation Concerning Marriage

1. Love one another: Love is your river of life . . . your eternal source of recreating yourselves. "Love never fails," says St. Paul.

"Love is worth more than all the wealth of your house," says the Song of Solomon.

"To love one another allows us to see God in each other, for when we love one another, God lives in us," says St. John.

2. Listen to one another: "Don't listen only for words . . . but for non-verbal language . . . body language . . . the language of tone, mood, and feelings."

"Learn to listen to one another . . . to understand one another, rather than listening to win an argument or a debate . . ."

3. Live with one another in friendship and partnership: "Friendship in marriage can be a peaceful island, separate and apart, in a world of turmoil and strife."

"When marriage is a partnership, no one is boss."

"When marriage is a partnership, we respect one another's rights and individuality."

"When marriage is a partnership, each is entitled to his or her own choices and mistakes."

"When marriage is a partnership, each is equal."

"And when we are both partners and friends in marriage, we can share the coming future years in tranquility and peace."

Declaration of Intention: Marriage has great possibility of success and failure as well as joy and pain. The possibility of sorrow and happiness is greater in married life than in single life. The person who has not made the wager of devotion cannot be hurt by another as can the person who puts his faith in another, nor can he know joy as the one who shares all with a trusted, loving companion.

(To Groom): ______________ , will you take ______________ as your wife; will you be faithful to her in tender love and honor, offering her strength, encouragement and companionship; and will you live with her, and cherish her, as love and respect would lead you, in the bonds of marriage?

Answer: I will.

(To Bride): ______________ , will you take ______________ as your husband; will you be faithful to him in tender love and honor, offering him strength, encouragement and companionship; and will you live with him, and cherish him, as love and respect would lead you, in the bonds of marriage?

Answer: I will.

Prayer: Let us pray: Out of this tangled world, O God, you have drawn together these two people and are binding them firmly by the sure insights of love. We thank you for the homes in which

______________ and ______________ have lived, for parents who have supported them and encouraged them even in the most trying times and who have sacrificed in their behalf and made great opportunities possible. We also thank you for the friendships they have enjoyed and for the church which has awakened them to the meaning of eternal life.

Our Father, bless this couple as they come before family, friends, and church to affirm the choice that they have made of each other. As we share with them in the celebration of love on this occasion, may we all grow toward the perfection that is experienced in your love. We pray in the Spirit of the Love of Christ. Amen

(Couple goes to the altar.)

Exchange of Vows: (Face one another) ______________ and ______________ , marriage requires a great deal of unselfishness, generosity, flexibility, patience and love from both husband and wife. Under it lies the responsibility of your home and community, but when it is supported by all the commitments of your love, these responsibilities do not weigh heavily. The realness and happiness of your marriage depend upon your love for each other and the strength of your commitment.

Rings: As a symbol of your commitment you have chosen these rings.

(To Groom) ______________ , will you place this ring upon the finger of your bride and give your promise to her?

Groom: ______________ , I take you to be my wife from this time onward, to join with you and to share all that is to come, to give and to receive, to speak and to listen, to inspire and to respond with love, and in all circumstances of our life together to be loyal to you with my whole life and with all my being so that together we may serve God and others as long as we both shall live.

(To Bride) ______________ , will you place this ring upon the finger of your groom and give your promise to him?

Bride: ______________ , I take you to be my husband from this time onward, to join with you and to share all that is to come, to give and to receive, to speak and to listen, to inspire and to respond with love, and in all circumstances of our life together to be loyal to you with my whole life and with all my being so that together we may serve God and others as long as we both shall live.

Lighting of the Unity Candle: (Symbolic of lives becoming one.)

Reading: From *The Prophet,* Kahlil Gibran, comes a passage which the bride and groom have chosen to enlighten all of us as to the essence of their love for one another, the love which they professed today before God, family and friends:

"Love one another, but make not a bond of love; Let it rather be a moving sea between the shores of your souls. Fill each other's cup but drink not from one cup. Give one another of your bread but eat not from the same loaf. Sing and dance together and be joyous, but let each one of you be alone, Even as the strings of a lute are alone though they quiver with the same music. Give your hearts, but not into each other's keeping. For only the hand of Life can contain your hearts. And stand together yet not too near together; For the pillars of the temple stand apart, And the oak tree and the cypress grow not in each other's shadow."*

Charge to the Couple: If marriage is to be maintained at a high level for both of you, this commitment must be practiced daily. Two people are not married in the ceremony; you only begin to be married. What is begun must continue with increasing meaning. The trials which married life encounters are great; only a strong commitment and spiritual motivation can maintain it. Mere physical attractiveness is not enough. Only the love of God will suffice.

(Couple kneels.)

The Lord's Prayer

Declaration of Marriage: Since you, _______________ and _______________ , have consented together to be married, and have witnessed the same before God and this community of relatives and friends and have committed love to and faith in each other and have sealed the promises with rings, I announce that God has made you husband and wife.

(Kiss)

Benediction: The Lord God who created our first parents and sanctified their union in marriage, sanctify and bless you, that you may please him both in body and soul and live together in holy love until life's end. Amen

*Reprinted from *The Prophet*, by Kahlil Gibran, by permission of Alfred A. Knopf, Inc.

18

Unique characteristics in this ceremony:

This service uses a traditional opening statement, traditional vows and words at the exchange of the rings, and the old English style is left intact — even in the statement of intent.

A contemporary prayer is inserted between the reading of the lessons, but the rest of the service, the solemnization of the marriage, the marriage blessing, and the benediction are all in Elizabethan English.

The marriage service of ______________ and ______________ on ______________ .

Invocation: In the name of the Father, and of the Son, and of the Holy Spirit. Amen

Who gives ______________ to be married to ______________ ?

Father responds: "Her mother and I."

Dearly Beloved: We are gathered together in the presence of God to witness and bless the joining of ______________ and ______________ in holy matrimony. The union of husband and wife in heart, body, and mind is intended by God for their mutual joy; for the help and comfort given one another in prosperity and in peril; and, when it is God's will, for the procreation of children and their nurture in the knowledge and love of the Lord. Therefore, marriage is not to be entered into unadvisedly or lightly, but reverently, deliberately, and in accordance with the purposes for which it was instituted by God.

Scripture Readings: The Lord God said: "It is not good that the man should be alone; I will make him a helper fit for him." So the Lord God caused a deep sleep to fall upon the man, and while he slept took one of his ribs and closed up its place with flesh. And the rib which the Lord God had taken from the man he made into a woman and brought her to the man. Then the man said, "This is bone of my bone and flesh of my flesh; she shall be called Woman, because she was taken out of Man." (Genesis 2:18, 21-23)

Our Lord Jesus Christ said: "From the beginning of creation

God made them male and female. For this reason a man shall leave his father and mother and be joined to his wife and the two shall become one. So they are no longer two, but one. What therefore God has joined together, let not man put asunder." (Mark 10:6-9)

Prayer: Let us pray: Out of all the human family, dear Father, you have drawn together these two individuals to unite them as one. We thank you for the homes in which ______________ and ______________ have been nurtured in the formative years of their lives; for parents who have sacrificed on their behalf and made possible opportunities of education; for the church which has awakened them to the meaning of eternal life. Our Father, bless these as they come before family, friends, and church to affirm the choices that they have made of each other as husband and wife and their intention to establish a home where your love may be celebrated in the family. Grant them the grace of faithfulness and true affection toward each other. For the fulfilment of their vows, may they discern the varied facets of your many-splendored love. May your Word nurture them all the days of their lives that their dreams and aspirations for life may find completeness in the doing of your will in all ways. As we share with them in the celebration of love on this occasion, may we all grow toward the perfection that is experienced in Christ our Lord. Amen

Scripture Readings: The Apostle Paul, speaking by the Holy Spirit, says: "Set your hearts on the greater gifts. I will show you the way which surpasses all the others. If I speak in the tongues of men and of angels, but have not love, I am a noisy gong or a clanging cymbal. And if I have prophetic powers, and understand all mysteries and all knowledge, and if I have all faith, so as to move mountains, but have not love, I am nothing. If I give away all I have, and if I deliver my body to be burned, but have not love, I gain nothing. Love is patient and kind; love is not jealous or boastful; it is not arrogant or rude. Love does not insist on its own way; it is not irritable or resentful; it does not rejoice at wrong, but rejoices in the right. Love bears all things, believes all things, hopes all things, endures all things. Love never ends." (1 Corinthians 12:31—13:8)

In the First Letter of John we read: "Beloved, let us love one another for love is of God, and he who loves is born of God and knows God. He who does not love does not know God; for God is love. In this, the love of God was made manifest among us, that God sent his only Son into the world, so that we might live through him. In this is love, not that we loved God, but that he loved us and sent his Son to be the expiation for our sins. Beloved, if God so loved us, we also ought to love one another. No man has ever seen God; if we love one another, God abides in us and his love is perfected in us." (1 John 4:7-12)

The Wedding Address: The Lord God in his goodness created us male and female, and by the gift of marriage founded human community in a joy that begins now and is brought to perfection in the life to come. These two, who have previously traveled separate ways, come now to be made one.

Statement of Intent: Do you, _____________ , take this woman to be thy wedded wife, to live together after God's Ordinance in the holy estate of matrimony? Wilt thou love her, comfort her, honor and keep her in sickness and in health, and, forsaking all others, keep thee only unto her, as long as you both shall live?" "If so, answer, "I do."

Do you, _____________ , take this man to be thy wedded husband, to live together after God's Ordinance in the holy estate of matrimony? Wilt thou love him, comfort him, honor and keep him in sickness and in health, and, forsaking all others, keep thee only unto him, as long as you both shall live? If so, answer, "I do."

(To altar.)

Marriage Vows: Join right hands and face each other — repeat after me:

(Groom) "I, _____________ , take thee, _____________ , to be my wedded wife, to have and to hold from this day forward, for better for worse, for richer for poorer, in sickness and in health, to love and to cherish, till death us do part."

(Bride) "I, _____________ , take thee, _____________ , to be my wedded husband, to have and to hold from this day forward, for better for worse, for richer for poorer, in sickness and in health, to love and to cherish, till death us do part."

Exchange of Rings: (To Groom) _____________ , take _____________ by the left hand, and placing the ring upon her finger, repeat after me:

"As a pledge and a token of the vows between us made, with this ring, I thee wed."

(To Bride) _____________ , take _____________ by the left hand, and placing the ring upon his finger, repeat after me:

"As a pledge and a token of the vows between us made, with this ring, I thee wed."

Solemnization of the Marriage: Forasmuch as _____________ and ______________ have consented together in holy wedlock and have declared the same before God and these witnesses, I now pronounce them husband and wife. In the name of the Father, and of the Son, and of the Holy Spirit. Amen

What God has joined together, let not man put asunder.

Lighting of the Unity Candle: ______________ and ______________ now symbolize their union by lighting a common candle. The two outside candles have been lit to represent two distinct lives, each capable of going its separate way. To bring happiness into their new home, there must be a merging of these two lights into one. As this one light cannot be divided, it is God's plan in Scripture that neither shall these lives be divided, but shall stand as a testimony of the unity that each can experience with Christ.

Marriage Blessing: (Kneel) The Lord God, who created our first parents and sanctified their union in marriage, sanctify and bless you, that you may please him both in body and soul and live together in Holy love until life's end. Amen

Prayer: Let us pray: Almighty and most merciful God, who hast now united this man and this woman in holy matrimony, grant them grace to live therein according to Thy Holy Word, strengthening them in constant fidelity, faith, and affection toward one another. In Jesus' Name. Amen

Benediction: And now may the Lord bless thee and keep thee. May the Lord make his face to shine upon thee and be gracious unto thee. The Lord lift up his countenance upon thee and give thee peace. In the name of the Father, and of the Son, and of the Holy Spirit. Amen

You may kiss the bride.

I now present to you Mr. and Mrs. ______________ ______________ !

19

Unique characteristics of this ceremony:

This last wedding service was the service of my daughter Kim and her husband Jeff Keisler. I escorted my daughter down the aisle, and then, during a solo, I entered the sacristy and joined my brother, Rev. August Homburg, and Jeff's grandfather, Dr. E. Bryan Keisler, in conducting the wedding.

The service combines the traditional with the contemporary. The lessons are both from the traditional Revised Standard Version and from contemporary translations.

The Benediction at the end is a prayer for the couple as well as a blessing.

The marriage service of ______________ and ______________ on ______________ .

Invocation: In the name of the Father and of the Son, and of the Holy Spirit. Amen

Prayer: Let us pray. O God, who alone unites persons in the Holy Bonds of Covenant, without whose Spirit there is no abiding unity or oneness, be present in the inner being of ______________ and ______________ who have come this day to witness to their commitment to each other, in the Spirit of the Love of Christ. Amen

Who gives ______________ to be married to ______________ ?

Father responds: "Her mother and I."

Statement Concerning Marriage: A wedding is the celebration of the highest we know in love, the pledging of two lives to become one. ______________ and ______________ , as you think about making your vows to each other, realize that henceforth your destinies will be woven together in such a pattern that sorrow for one will be sorrow for the other and that joy for one will be joy for the other. This evening you will commit yourselves to each other to give support and love in all times. The words, "I love you," first spoken shyly in months gone by, will now be spoken in full commitment of yourselves to each other. Always remember the love you share is God's gift. "We love because God first loved us," for "God is Love."

Lessons: Listen to what the Word of God teaches concerning marriage:

The Lord God said: "It is not good that man should be alone, I will make a helper fit for him." (Genesis 2:18)

Our Lord Jesus Christ said: "From the beginning of creation God made them male and female. For this reason a man shall leave his father and mother and be joined to his wife, and the two shall become one. So they are no longer two, but one. What therefore God has joined together, let not man put asunder." (Mark 10:6-9)

The Apostle Paul speaking by the Holy Spirit says: "I may speak in the tongues of men or of angels, but if I am without love, I am a sounding gong or a clanging cymbal. I may have the gift of prophecy, and know every hidden truth, I may have faith strong enough to move mountains, but if I have no love, I am nothing. I may dole out all I possess, or even give my body to be burned, but if I have no love, I am none the better. Love is patient, love is kind and envies no one. Love is never boastful, nor conceited, nor rude, never selfish, not quick to take offense. Love keeps no score of wrongs, does not gloat over other's sins, but delights in the truth. There is nothing love cannot face, there is no limit to its faith, its hope, and its endurance. Love never ends. Are there prophets? Their work will be over. Are there outbursts of ecstasy? They will cease. Is there knowledge? It will vanish away. For our knowledge and our prophecy are but partial, and the partial vanishes when wholeness comes. When I was a child, my speech, my outlook, and my thoughts were all childish. When I grew up, I had finished with childish things. Now we see puzzling reflections in a mirror, but then we shall see face to face. In a word, there are three things that last forever, faith, hope, and love, but the greatest of them all is love." (1 Corinthians 13:1-13)

In the First Letter of St. John we read: "Beloved, let us love one another, for love is of God, and whoever loves is born of God and knows God. Whoever does not love does not know God, for God is love. In this the love of God was made manifest among us, that God sent his only Son into the world so that we might live through him. In this is love, not that we loved God, but that he loved us and sent his Son to be the expiation for our sins. Beloved, if God so loved us, we also ought to love one another. No one has ever seen God, but if we love one another, we see God abiding in us and we in him." (1 John 4:7-12)

Meditation: ______________ and ______________ , we are all made by God to love and be loved. We walk this earth as unfinished creations until we find fulfilment in the knowledge of God's love for us in Jesus Christ and God's love in one another. You were both very fortunate, for in your early infancy you were baptized into God's Kingdom of Love. In your childhood and early years you shared your joys and fears, your triumphs and sorrows in the love of your parents and your sisters. Emerging into maturity, the hunger of lonely souls brought you to the greatest thing in human life, the love God gives us to share as man and woman. In your sharing of your love, you have become complete and finished creations. In your marriage, the fusion of two persons into one new creation, you will find completeness and divine fulfilment in holy love.

______________ and ______________ , as you each sacrifice some freedom to the covenant between you that makes you one, you will find freedom from loneliness and self-concern. As you pledge exclusive devotion to each other, you will find a flood of tenderness welling up within you, which can become a passion for the welfare of all humanity. As you share your innermost love with each other, you will find that God is dwelling in your midst. We are all very happy for you both, for you have found the key that unlocks the universe, and that is love.

1. Have faith — trust in each other.
2. Have hope in each other.
3. Love each other — as God loves us.

Prayer: Loving Heavenly Father: You ordained marriage for your children, ______________ and ______________ . You gave them love. And now we present them to you to be married. May their union be blessed with true devotion, spiritual commitment, and unselfish love. Loving God, give them the power and strength to keep the covenant they will make between them. When selfishness shows itself, grant generosity; when there is misunderstanding, give them patience and gentleness; when there is wrong-doing, give them a forgiving spirit; and when suffering becomes their lot, give them a strong faith and abiding hope. In the name of our loving Lord and Savior Jesus Christ. Amen

Statement of Intention: Do you, ______________ , take ______________ to be your wedded wife, to live together after God's ordinance in the Holy Estate of Matrimony? Will you love her, comfort her, honor and keep her in sickness and in health, and forsaking all others, keep only unto her, as long as you both shall live?

Groom: "I do."

______________ , do you take ______________ to be your wedded husband, to live together after God's ordinance in the Holy Estate of Matrimony? Will you love him, comfort him, honor and keep him in sickness and in health, and forsaking all others, keep only unto him, as long as you both shall live?

Bride: "I do."

(Couple goes to the altar.)

Vows: I, ______________ , take you, ______________ , to be my wedded wife, to have and to hold, from this day forward, for better for worse, for richer for poorer, in sickness and in health, to love and to cherish, until death do us 'part.

I, ______________ , take you, ______________ , to be my wedded husband, to have and to hold, from this day forward, for better for worse, for richer for poorer, in sickness and in health, to love and to cherish, until death do us part.

Blessing of Rings: Lord, bless these rings, in the name of the Father and of the Son, and of the Holy Spirit. Grant that ______________ and ______________ who wear them, may always have a deep faith in each other. May they do your will and always live together in peace, goodwill, and love. We ask this through Christ our Lord. Amen

Groom: (Places ring on bride's finger and says:) "As this ring has no end, neither shall my love for you."

Bride: (Places ring on groom's finger and says:) "As this ring has no end, neither shall my love for you."

Lighting of the Unity Candle: Now that you, ______________ and ______________ , have given yourselves to each other by your solemn vows and the exchanging of rings, symbolize your union by lighting the wedding candle as a sign that you are no longer two, but one. May your love burn bright and may your life together be a light, an example of Christ's love in the world.

(Song is sung during lighting of unity candle, and couple presents flowers to their mothers.)

Pronouncement of Marriage: For as much as ______________ and ______________ have consented together in holy wedlock and have declared the same before God and these witnesses, I pronounce them husband and wife, and in the name of the Father, and of the Son, and of the Holy Spirit. Amen

What God has joined together, let not man put asunder.

(Couple kneels.)

Marriage Blessing: The Lord God who created our first parents and established them in marriage, establish and sustain you, that you may find delight in each other and grow in Holy Love until your life's end. May you dwell in God's presence forever and may true and constant love preserve you. Amen.

Prayer: Father of love, shower your grace upon ______________ and ______________ who have come before you and pledged themselves to live together in love, in the covenant of holy marriage. Give them wisdom and devotion in the ordering of their common life that each may be to the other a strength in need, a counselor in perplexity, a comforter in sorrow, and a companion in joy. Give them such fulfilment in their mutual affection for each other that they may reach out in love and concern for others. Grant that all married persons who have witnessed these vows may find their lives strengthened and their loyalties confirmed. In Christ's name. Amen

The Lord's Prayer

Benediction: Eternal God of love, without your grace no promise is sure. Strengthen ______________ and ______________ with the gift of your spirit so that they may fulfill the vows they have taken. Keep them faithful to each other and to you. Fill them with such love and joy that they may build a home where no one is a stranger. And guide them by your Word and strengthen them with your sacraments so that they may serve you all the days of their lives. Through Jesus Christ our Lord, to whom be honor and glory, forever and forever.

And now may the joy and peace which only God can give and which cannot be taken away by anything in this world, be yours today and in all of life's tomorrows, in the name of the Father and of the Son and of the Holy Spirit. Amen

(Kiss the bride.)

Scripture Index

Text	*Service(s)*
Genesis 1:26-31a	6, 7, 16
Genesis 2:18	1, 15, 17, 19
Genesis 2:18, 21-24	4, 13, 15, 18
Psalm 33	5
Song of Solomon 2:10-13	17
Matthew 19:4-6	7
Mark 10:6-9	1, 6, 17, 18, 19
John 15:12-16	16
1 Corinthians 12:31—13:8	1, 18
1 Corinthians 13	2, 3, 4, 7, 8, 15, 17, 19
Ephesians 5:21-33	5, 10, 13, 14, 17, 18, 19